Your Best Trip Ever!

YOUR BEST TRIP EVER!

PLAN, TAKE, AND SHARE TRIPS TO AMERICA'S NATIONAL PARKS AND MORE

BRIAN PHELPS

iUniverse®

YOUR BEST TRIP EVER!
PLAN, TAKE, AND SHARE TRIPS TO AMERICA'S NATIONAL PARKS AND MORE

iUniverse books may be ordered through booksellers or by contacting:

iUniverse
1663 Liberty Drive
Bloomington, IN 47403
www.iuniverse.com
1-800-Authors (1-800-288-4677)

ISBN: 978-1-4917-5614-0 (sc)
ISBN: 978-1-4917-5613-3 (e)

Library of Congress Control Number: 2015900985

Printed in the United States of America.

iUniverse rev. date: 2/13/2015

To MY PARENTS for putting up with me all these years and coming with us on the awesome eastern odyssey.

And to my wife and two sons for also putting up with me all these years and sharing these many incredible experiences with a minimum of yelling.

CONTENTS

Color copies of these photographs available online at
http://www.ephelps.com/bookxx.htm.

PROLOGUE

What excites you? What really excites you? The birth of a child? A family milestone? A career achievement? A sports victory or championship? Me too. What else excites you? A personal hobby? One that you like to talk about? One you are passionate about? One that you think about often? One that you like to do as often as possible? One that might spur others to follow your path? Me too. As my kids have grown, one of the hobbies my family has embraced is travel. In recent times, travel to national parks and national monuments has brought us countless memories. There are thousands of books and endless information sources online about our beautiful national treasures, and many of them can help you mold a fantastic trip. My intention is not to try to provide you with an exhaustive technical guide to all of these locations. I want to have a conversation and share with you my family's unique trip itineraries, providing you with a reference and ideas to plan and enjoy your best trip ever. I get excited just thinking about these places. I want you to get so excited that hopefully you will even get to plan and take three, four, or more best trips ever.

I remember talking to a younger parent at a pool in Mystic, Connecticut, about our travels to that point. He told me his goal was to get to all of the national parks while his kids were still at home. I agreed this was a laudable idea, but it is also very tough to do. Available vacation time, ages, fitness levels, finances, kids' schedules, spouse's schedules, geography, and other factors may or may not let you even think about such a lofty goal. My experiences have taken the reality of our situation to pack in as much quality travel time as possible. I waited to take these major outdoors trips until I was comfortable with my sons' ages, knowing then that we would not have to look after them twenty-four hours a day. This book will chronicle the six major trips my family has taken from 2006 to 2014.

- chapter 1—Yellowstone, Badlands, and Zion National Parks (2006)
- chapter 2—Grand Canyon, Arches, and Bryce Canyon National Parks (2008)
- chapter 3—Acadia National Park and Bar Harbor, Maine (2009)
- chapter 4—Olympic and Glacier National Parks (2010)
- chapter 5—Yosemite, Death Valley, and Zion National Parks (2012)
- chapter 6—the lost Utah national parks and monuments (2014)

Some of the trips built on earlier trips, but each one can be planned as a unique adventure, open to changes that can make it even better. My objectives have been simple. I wanted to

- have fun planning a vacation;
- have even more fun taking the vacation;
- capture memories and stories that would bring joy and laughter to you in the future;
- get others excited about the places where we have been so they hopefully follow in our footsteps; and
- plan to return some day.

Our excursions have actually spurred friends to take similar journeys to some of the same places. If I can get you to do the same (maybe even taking the exact same route), this effort will have been a success to me. If you want me to help you plan or even go along, let me know. I would love to.

A Little Personal Travel History

As a young child in the 1970s, I traveled with my family from Michigan to numerous locations in the East, Midwest, and South. We packed into the Bonneville or Chevy station wagon and went to Gettysburg, Amish country, Washington, DC, Williamsburg, the

Great Smoky Mountains National Park, Rock City, Myrtle Beach, Shenandoah National Park, Gatlinburg, Jamestown, Knoxville, Sleeping Bear Dunes National Lakeshore, Oscoda, and Mammoth Onyx Cave, just to name a few places. We are a large family, and air-conditioning was not always available; however, we benefited from my parents' meticulous planning. I look back fondly on these trips, even the beer can hunting episode, and they planted seeds in me so that I wanted to learn about and explore more of our great country.

After I graduated from Central Michigan University, I began my career in the late 1980s. Different jobs took me to Dallas, New York City, and Detroit. While I was living alone in these far off places, I was generally too busy working to travel much or enjoy the scenery. Then I got married and eventually settled in Bay City, Michigan, near my hometown of Saginaw. As my wife and I remodeled a one hundred-year-old house (I did all the work) before the boys were born, we traveled. We went to places farther away than I had been on prior trips. We took weeklong trips, driving to the coast of Maine and Acadia National Park in 1992 and to New Orleans in 1993. The Maine trip was my first real big trip-planning experience, and I researched it with my wife, planning extensively. This was before the Internet, so atlases, travel agencies, chambers of commerce, and mailed travel guides were the order of the day. Boothbay Harbor and Bar Harbor were fantastically beautiful at the end of May, and we became honorary members of the Sunrise Club on top of Cadillac Mountain. I also ate the largest swordfish steak I have ever seen, and we were sailors on a schooner. We survived our exhaust pipe falling off at the top of Cadillac Mountain, and we found a great little garage in Seal Cove to fix it for us. In the days before digital cameras, I also discovered my penchant for photography mishaps that continue to this day. The drive home took us through New Hampshire, the Green Mountains and the Long Trail Brewery in Vermont, and the town of Phelps, New York. They had never heard of us. As soon as we left Maine, I was already planning to return someday. In New Orleans, we were pregnant with our first child. Because of this, my wife would take a nap each afternoon in our room at the Hotel de la Poste on Chartres Street in the French Quarter. I would then go down to a corner bar and drink a couple of Dixies or Blackened Voodoos. Yummy. We encountered gators in the swamp, toured the French Quarter and the waterfront, and ate gumbo, crawfish, jambalaya, poboys, and muffulettas.

Our first son was born in early 1994 (my wife did most of the work), and in late summer, we felt he was old enough to endure us being away for a week. So we flew out to Seattle, Washington. While we were potentially trying to do too much in one trip, we packed a great deal of fun into a short week. We had dinner at the top of the Space Needle, shopped at Pike Place Fish Market, ferried around Puget Sound, attended the Great Northwest Microbrewery Invitational craft beer festival, toured the Rainier Brewery, visited Snoqualmie Falls and Mount Saint Helens, and ate at Ivar's Salmon House. We enjoyed the beautiful Cascades mountain range, and we drove counterclockwise around Mount Rainier National Park. This is where I discovered my fear of falling off the side of a cliff while driving around a mountain with no guardrails. However, when we stopped the vehicle, I managed to enjoy the tremendous beauty of the mountain as our heads were literally in the clouds. It took me a long time to regain the ability to drive mountain roads without freezing, though it never went away completely. Later in 1994, we attended a convention in Orlando, Florida, where I had a speaking engagement. We flew with our nine-month-old son, and fortunately he traveled pretty well. We had a great time at the Universal Studios theme park, but our stroller-bound son was somewhat traumatized by a large costumed cartoon character. I am sure it did not mean him any harm. *This was a pivotal moment for me in thinking about future trips alone with the family. Should we go to cartoon theme parks or see the great outdoors?*

My second son was born in late 1996, and we were again busy with work and a newborn. Our traveling was held to a minimum. Near the end of 1998, I took a new job, and we moved to a suburb of Pittsburgh, Pennsylvania. While we were leaving our home state, we settled into a place that would become a great central location for many excursions within reasonable driving distance. Eventual trips to Niagara Falls, Charleston (South Carolina), New York City, Washington, DC, Presque Isle (Pennsylvania), North Manchester (Indiana), Chicago, Frankenmuth, Virginia Beach, Fort Mill (South Carolina), Indianapolis, and back home to Michigan were all memorable and reasonable destinations without having to fly.

In 2002, I had accumulated enough miles on my credit card to obtain plane tickets for all four of us. This led to our first weeklong family trip. We wanted to visit old friends in Southern California. We also wanted to visit the headquarters of my wife's dance-fitness company in Carlsbad. We also wanted to take the kids to Legoland, Disneyland, and the Anaheim Pond. We also wanted to play on the ocean beaches in San Diego and see Malibu and Hollywood. We also wanted to eat good food. Well, we packed all of these things into that week. Fortunately the kids enjoyed flying, and we had a great time.

This trip introduced key concepts I would use for the really big trips to come. Most of them become apparent to you when you are planning a trip, and their value increases when they are applied together.

- While other countries are great destinations I may try to see some day, the United States has many awesome places to experience with relative ease.
- Plan, coordinate, and reserve well in advance. Be prepared for modifications and unexpected changes.
- Pick the central location you want to get to, and branch out from there to find more places you would like to experience.
- Do and see as much as you can in the time that you have, but strive to spend quality time at the place(s) you really want to see.
- Try to see new places and do new things each time you travel. Even if you only get a few moments to see something or someplace, it can leave a lasting impression and is better than never experiencing it at all.
- Learn the geography, terrain, and weather patterns of your destinations.
- When you are planning the driving, choose routes with as much beauty and history as possible while you balance driving time with sightseeing time.
- Decide at what age(s) you are comfortable with your kids embracing activities in new environments, such as national parks and forests.
- Choose activities that are appropriate for the kids' ages, that you will all enjoy, and that you can participate in with low stress.

- Choose activities you want to do that the kids would also enjoy, using child bribery when necessary and within reason.
- Get yourselves into decent shape. Exercise before the trip to build up stamina.
- Take as many vacation days as possible, but if you only have a week of vacation time because of family constraints, extend the time off by leaving really early on Saturday and coming home late the following Sunday.
- Take advantage of time zone changes, and try to avoid times when places get really crowded (holidays, high season, etc.).
- Budget within your means for the trip, and spread the costs out over time.
- Visit friends/family whenever feasible. If possible, stay with them to defray costs.
- Use accumulated flight rewards miles to reduce costs even further, but be wary of restrictions. (Remember to try and pay off the credit card while amassing miles.) This is a great cost-saver, but do not let the cost of transportation stop you from seeing far-off places, particularly out west.
- Don't overspend on food, but don't skimp either. You will remember awesome meals and the stinkers too.
- Take the best electronic gear you can afford to record your adventures so you can revisit and share them time and time again.
- Do activities that will produce memories and stories that you can enjoy telling and retelling.
- Sample and enjoy local foods (fish, fruits, etc.) and beverages (craft beers, wine, etc.) as often as possible.
- Always try to find a silver lining if a trip event does not go just how you planned or hoped.

Now that we had been "out west," I knew I wanted to go back. It was only a matter of time.

CHAPTER 1: THE FIRST ODYSSEY
THE FIRST NATIONAL PARK (2006)

PREPARATIONS

Back in 2005, my boys were eight and eleven. They were active and athletic and liked being outside. We had traveled with them to many locations, mostly over long weekends and within four to seven hours of drive time. I started to think about finally taking another weeklong vacation, and I felt good about the boys getting into more advanced outdoor adventures. My trips to Maine and Washington states (before children) rekindled the desire to experience the parks and the great locations within these United States. It was then that I looked again to the West and to the national parks and monuments. There were so many to choose from, but I finally settled on "America's First National Park." Yellowstone National Park was the perfect choice.

We also wanted to meet up with our friends from Southern California again, so we decided the final destination for the trip would be Las Vegas. Now Las Vegas is a long way from Yellowstone, so I had to build in time for at least one really long driving day with a stop in between. I wanted to stay several days in Yellowstone, so the eight or nine total days of vacation time were dwindling already.

What you need to realize is the planning (the journey) can be as fun and rewarding as the actual trip (the destination). In retrospect, I wish we could have taken two or more weeks off and had a lot more money to spend, but these were not luxuries we had at our disposal. Thus, since I had the main destination and the final destination, it was time to branch out

1

and see what else we could experience affordably in nine days. Extensive Internet research using the National Park Service website, the sites of the parks, state websites, and atlases provided abundant information. Many parks also publish periodicals that provide timely information covering all aspects of your visit there. I focused on national parks and monuments, picking the ones that we could fit in and hopefully enjoy the most together. I used to sit in business meetings and draw maps of the western United States, tracing the routes I wanted to take to the places I wanted to visit. I kept molding the places, dates, times, etc. Often initial plans will change, and some places will be ruled out, while others will be added as the masterpiece takes shape. This is all part of the learning and fun of the planning process. Arm yourself with maps and a calendar … and let's go.

Step one was choosing when we would go. Because of the kids' schedules, we chose the middle of July. While this is generally the warmest time of the year in the West, the average temperature in Yellowstone is still only around 70 degrees. Plus, the humidity is relatively low, so higher temperatures are more tolerable, even in Las Vegas. It can also snow in late spring and even in summer, so waiting gives you better odds that all of the roads are open. You trade off some of the beauty of winter and the spring thaw for drivability and open passages.

Step two was figuring out a very important part of planning the trip. "How would we get there?" I originally thought about driving from Pennsylvania, but the realization that using half of the trip just for this would be a waste. Fortunately I had once again saved up enough miles on my credit card to get four airline tickets for free. *This became the fundamental building block for all of our trips out west. We would use miles to fly for free and rent a vehicle while we were out there.* I recommend this approach, but not everyone has miles saved up on a credit card. This is where you have to weigh the cost of flights and realize it could add a few thousand dollars to the overall cost. Don't let this deter you though, as the destinations are well worth seeing. Driving or trains can take a lot of time too, but if you can take more than a week off, they can be a cheaper alternative to flying and offer many more experiences along the way. Of course, if you already live in the western half of the country, then you are in a great position to get to these locations with much less effort.

Step three was determining where we were going to visit and on what days. I sometimes try to do too much, and one original thought was to go to the Mall of America in Minnesota and spend a day there prior to Yellowstone. I quickly ruled this out, as it would have added a lot of driving time and subtracted time from Yellowstone. Years ago when we flew to Seattle, we flew over the Badlands and grasslands of South Dakota. I could see the moonscape from the airplane, and I told myself I needed to visit there some day. This was not that far from Yellowstone, so it would become our first stop, and I am so happy it did. It is also near Mount Rushmore, and this allowed me to inject some historical sightseeing for the kids. Using my frequent flyer miles, I was able to book flights to the airport in Rapid City, South Dakota. The Badlands are about seventy-five miles east of Rapid City across I-90. While I was plotting the course from the Black Hills of South Dakota to Yellowstone, I found some really great places in between. Devils Tower National Monument in Wyoming and Little Bighorn National Battlefield in Montana were in close proximity of I-90. Count them in! And that was just Sunday. From there it was on to Yellowstone for three days. Since our ultimate destination was a meeting with friends in Las Vegas, I needed one more stop in between Yellowstone and Vegas. We were traveling through Utah, and Salt Lake City was somewhere in the middle. However, I wanted another national park. This is where Zion National Park entered the plan. It was conveniently right off I-15 in southwestern Utah. Sure, it was almost 750 miles from Yellowstone, but I was pretty sure I could keep the kids happy for twelve or thirteen hours in the car. At least I hoped so. Thursday was pegged as the "big drive" day. So the trip route was set—the Badlands and Deadwood on Saturday; Mount Rushmore, Devils Tower, and Bighorn Battlefield on Sunday; Yellowstone on Monday through Wednesday; Zion on Thursday night and Friday morning; and Las Vegas on Friday evening and Saturday! *This was going to be the best trip ever!* At least up until that point.

Step four was determining where we were going to stay. When you think of traveling to parks, camping might come to mind. I realize some people enjoy getting rained on in the cold without a real shower, but not me. I did do some camping when I was younger, and I generally enjoyed it. I enjoyed Copper Harbor and Tahquamenon Falls in

Michigan's Upper Peninsula, lost the feeling in my body swimming in Lake Superior, and I roughed it in Heber Springs, Arkansas. However, I endured some fairly traumatic experiences, but I had funny stories nonetheless. I made the early decision that whenever possible I wanted to stay in lodging in the national parks we were going to visit. If there was no lodging available, I wanted to stay at historic places. Chain hotels/motels would come last. For many of the national parks there are lodging operators that you contact to reserve rooms inside the park. Xanterra Parks and Resorts was the operator for Yellowstone and Zion in 2006 (and they still are), so we used their services to book rooms and schedule activities and meals. The town of Deadwood was in the vicinity of the Badlands and Mount Rushmore, and its western reputations appealed to me. I found the historic Franklin Hotel in Deadwood for our first night of lodging. The Hampton Inn in Billings, Montana, provided a nice place to relax before we headed to Yellowstone. Grant Village in Yellowstone had available rooms through Xanterra, and it had other amenities that turned out to be very convenient. The Zion Park Lodge was the only place to stay in Zion, and staying there allowed us to drive our vehicle into the park. Otherwise we would have to park outside and take the shuttle into the park. Excalibur Hotel in Las Vegas was family-friendly, so we would meet our friends and their two daughters there. Plus it was on the south end of the strip and right across from the airport, though the trip time to the airport can be deceptive. It is important to determine availability very early, as this can alter your trip before you get out of the gate. Use travel websites, search, call, and read the fine print, particularly regarding cancellation rules. For any of the lodging that is available through websites that offer rewards for booking through them, I recommend setting up accounts to accumulate free nights or whatever else is available.

Step five was adding tours and additional activities on to the location visits. The two places where we would be staying more than one day were Yellowstone and Las Vegas. In Yellowstone, many activities were available for review and booking online, and Xanterra's website was very helpful here. They control reservations for lodging, activities, meals, tours, etc., so this was a great place to start. Knowing that we would be coming in the north entrance late Monday morning, we decided on the

Old West Cookout in the Roosevelt area. We also reserved a bus for the all-day "Circle of Fire" tour on Tuesday to get good coverage of the more popular and well-known features of Yellowstone. On Wednesday, we chose the "Saddle Up" horseback riding tour in the morning followed by a two- to four-hour chartered fishing trip on Lake Yellowstone in the afternoon. This would keep us busy and hopefully keep the kids happy. In Las Vegas, I wanted to get to a couple of family-friendly shows, so we chose the Blue Man Group and King Arthur's Tournament and Joust.

Step six was choosing certain meals to get a little fancy with. Many trip meals are impromptu and may just be fast food. In the parks, however, I wanted to experience some of their dining facilities. While we already had the Chuck Wagon Dinner planned Monday night in Yellowstone, we also made reservations at the Old Faithful Inn and Grant Village Lake House restaurants the next two nights. I must say that these were very good choices. In Zion, the choice was easy. We would enjoy the Zion Lodge Red Rock Grill.

Step seven was choosing what vehicle we would drive around in. We wanted an all-wheel-drive vehicle that was decent on gas. Since our rental car pickup was occurring at the Rapid City airport, the vehicle selection was relatively less than major airports. I knew it was going to cost more because we were not dropping the car off at the same place, so I balanced utility and costs in making the choice.

Step eight was making sure we had the right supplies, gear, eyewear, and clothing. Key aspects of this step include your electronics, gadgets, sundries, outerwear, and shoes. Try not to overpack or underpack, but make sure you have durable hiking shoes. We chose Merrell shoes, but Columbia, Keen, Adidas, and North Face all make good rugged shoes.

Step nine was budgeting for the Great Western Odyssey. The worksheet below was taken right out of the spreadsheet file I have used for all of our major trips. It shows the schedule, locations, activities, prepaid costs, total estimated costs, and the timing of the payments for each item based on credit card billing cycles. It also estimates the miles to be driven in each segment, allowing me to estimate the fuel cost. My goal was to spread out the costs over time as much as possible. Costs obviously change over the years, so using the grid as a guideline will allow you to research current costs.

Brian Phelps

		2006 TRAVEL COSTS FOR OUR FUN				
DATES	DESTINATION	ITEM	COST	PREPAID COST	VISA PD MO	MILES
07/06	Western swing	Flights—additional costs	100.00	100.00	02/06	
07/06	Western swing	Deadwood Hotel—07/08/06	125.00		07/06	300
07/06	Western swing	Billings Hotel—07/09/06	125.00		07/06	500
07/06	Western swing	Yellowstone Lodging 07/10/06-07/12/06—Deposit	129.32	129.32	03/06	350
07/06	Western swing	Yellowstone Lodging 07/10/06-07/12/06—Balance	275.00		08/06	
07/06	Western swing	Zion Lodge 07/13/06—Full Deposit	154.73	154.73	03/06	675
07/06	Western swing	Vegas—Excalibur 07/14/06-07/15/06—Deposit	141.65	141.65	03/06	175
07/06	Western swing	Vegas—Excalibur 2 nights—Balance	125.00		08/06	
07/06	Western swing	Car Rental 07/08/06-07/16/06	737.00		08/06	
07/06	Western swing	Blue Man Group—07/14/06 (7:30 p.m.—Venetian)	504.00	504.00	05/06	
07/06	Western swing	King Arthur's Show—07/15/06 (8:30 p.m.—Excalibur)	489.92		07/06	
07/06	Western swing	Meals estimate 07/08-07/11 (est. $75/day)	300.00		07/06	
07/06	Western swing	Meals estimate 07/12-07/16 (est. $75/day)	375.00		08/06	
07/06	Western swing	Tours estimate 07/08-07/11 ($201.76+$130 so far)	350.00		07/06	
07/06	Western swing	Tours estimate 07/12-07/16 ($137.28+$148.40 so far)	300.00		08/06	
07/06	Western swing	Gas	120.00		07/06	
07/06	Western swing	Gas	180.00		08/06	
07/06	Western swing	Cash—Initial	400.00		Cash	
07/06	Western swing	Cash—ATMs on trip	200.00		Cash	
07/06	Western swing	Parking—Airport 07/16/06	79.00		Cash	

July	1,509.92	Totals	$5,210.62	$1,029.70		2,000
August	1,992.00			Prepaid		
Prepaid	1,029.70					
Cash	679.00					
	5,210.62					

THE TRIP

The excitement built in me for nearly a year, and now it was July 2006. Our flight out of Pittsburgh was early morning on the eighth. Getting up that early was not so bad, and we had time to sleep on the planes. Plus, we gained two hours over the time zones, so we still had a large chunk of daylight to work with. We arrived in South Dakota at the Rapid City airport late morning, and it was sunny and over 100 degrees. This was not a large airport, so getting our bags was easy. The rental car counter was also easy to get to, and we set out to make our vehicle choice. After some discussions we chose a Subaru Outback. We headed east out of the airport on I-90. Unlike many Western Pennsylvania roads, I-90 is generally straight and flat. It was a great ride. About an hour later we stopped outside Badlands National Park in Wall, South Dakota. Wall is a small town, but it has a massive tourist attraction called the Wall Drug Store. This seventy-six-thousand-square-foot adventure has something for everyone, and it was a welcome pit stop before our first hiking experience. We relaxed and browsed for a while, and then we drove into the park. For a trip where you are visiting multiple national parks, I recommend looking at a National Park Service annual park pass. If not, each park is generally around twenty-five dollars for a one-week pass.

Badlands is near the Minuteman Missile National Historic Site, and I initially wanted to see this. However, I also wanted some sunlight to walk around Deadwood, so we had to skip it this time around. Heading south out of Wall, we took the Highway 240 Badlands Loop Road. This is a forty-mile road that takes you through the northern section of the park. There is much more you can see in the park, but working within a time limit, it gives you a paved road through beautiful landscapes with a multitude of places to stop and enjoy the scenery. The forty-five-mile-per-hour road is well maintained, and going from west to east takes you to the nice visitor center. We stopped numerous times, and we did some hiking, climbing, and exploring. There are exhibits to explain the rock formations and history, and we saw a number of animals out during the hot, dry day. The National Park Service has a downloadable park guide newsletter that is very informative regarding all aspects of your Badlands visit. Of all the possible animals to see, we did see some bighorn sheep and prairie dogs. We also heard a rattle sound near a boardwalk that had signs warning of rattlesnakes. We stayed on the boardwalk. We spent several hours driving the loop road, stopping to climb and take pictures. The colorful markings on the mountains were really cool, and there were plenty of opportunities to hike and explore. We ended at the visitor center, taking a personal break before heading to our hotel. While I can say, "I was there," I realize that the Badlands has much more to experience than a few hours gave us, so I have been hoping to go back ever since. Some day I definitely will.

Badlands National Park

Now it was on to the Franklin Hotel in Deadwood, South Dakota. There are many places to stay in and around Deadwood, but I wanted to stay somewhere historic, so I chose the Franklin. We had about two hours to drive from the Badlands northeast entrance, and we got to the hotel shortly after six o'clock in the evening. We drove up Main Street and parked out front. We unloaded and checked in. Like many other buildings along Main Street, the Franklin has a casino on the main floor. It has mostly slot machines, and the kids enjoyed wandering around for a while. The room was nice and comfortable. I have read that the Franklin has upgraded since 2006, so I assume it is even nicer. After we got settled, we walked back down Main Street, passing casinos, bars, and restaurants. We found a small restaurant where we could enjoy burgers and fries outside. It was a nice end to a busy first day.

Sunday morning was time to head west. What is really cool about the Black Hills is there are many places to experience, and this area of South Dakota could be a great trip all by itself. We passed up Sturgis, Custer, Lead, Wind Cave, Jewel Cave, the Buffalo Gap Grassland, and the Black Hills National Forest. We did, however, head south to Mount Rushmore for our first adventure of the day. We stopped in Keystone outside the monument to get situated and refresh ourselves, and then it was on to Rushmore. You can see the massive presidents' heads from the highway as you are nearing the entrance, but you really have to go in to get the full effect. The entrance takes you into a walkway where flags fly overhead, and you start to take in the enormity of the monument project.

07/09/2006

Mount Rushmore National Memorial

The stone that was blasted off the mountain face all those years ago is sloped in a giant pile in front of the four heads. There is a walking trail that is not too long, and it gives you many good vantage points to view the heads from. There is a small museum, and the hike is not strenuous. You learn the history and see something really interesting. We spent a few hours at the monument, though we could easily have stayed longer. Now it was time to head to Wyoming.

As we were traveling Highway 16 from South Dakota northwest into Wyoming, we also drove by the Crazy Horse Monument. Similar in scope to Rushmore, it is an ongoing and massive carving out of the side of a mountain. We did not stop, but it was a really cool sight from the highway. Again a Black Hills excursion will hopefully be in my future, and this would likely be a part of it.

As you travel, you do little things that end up being the stuff of future memory along with the big events and locations. We drove through the nice little town of Upton, Wyoming, and apparently I was speeding. I was pulled over by the local sheriff. Fortunately the kids stayed under control in the back, and somehow I managed to avoid a ticket. No wonder the town's slogan is "The best town on earth." Sunday morning I agreed as I said "Thank you, Sheriff." We celebrated by stopping for lunch at a regional Mexican fast-food restaurant. That was probably a mistake, as you can imagine what a bunch of bean burritos can do to three men and a babe.

Now it was on to Devils Tower. We made our way up to I-90, and instead of heading west toward our final destination of Billings, Montana, we headed north into the wilderness. About forty-five minutes after Highway 16 intersects with I-90 past grasslands, forests, and rock formations, an amazing geological formation appears. It rose out of the ground long ago, and it is a fantastic sight. There may be UFOs on the top, but around the base is a series of trails and rocks just waiting to be experienced. We spent time hiking the trail around the mountain, enjoying trees and the occasional climbers at different heights on the side of the mountain. Since the boys liked to climb and explore, we all started to make our way toward the base of the mountain.

07/09/2006

Devils Tower National Monument

Large rock piles blown off the mountain made for a lot of fun as we slowly navigated the terrain. We were careful not to rush our ascent, and there were times when one of us would disappear from view into a crevasse or on the other side of a boulder. We took pictures and gazed up and down the mountain. We also walked a trail around part of the mountain, marveling at the continuous horizontal rock formations making up the tower. We even saw some climbers who were right near the top of the mountain. After our physical encounter, the visitor center was a nice place to rest and refresh. Around midafternoon we were on our way again. Overall we stayed here for a couple of hours, and I marked down yet another place I wanted to return to someday.

We still had a long drive ahead of us to our final stop in Billings, and after the forty-five-minute jaunt down to I-90, it was two hundred miles to Bighorn. Fortunately the speed limit was seventy-five, and I pushed it even higher toward the highway number. Sometimes the drive is mundane, but I like to look for different things as we go. One of the really cool things we saw in Wyoming was the trains. Wyoming is a big energy-producing state, and we saw some of the longest trains we had ever seen. Off in the distance trains with hundreds of cars were snaked parallel to the highway. We tried to count cars, and I estimated their lengths by timing how long it took to pass one from beginning to end. Some were miles long. We made great time and stopped for gas and a snack near the border of Montana in Sheridan, Wyoming. It was early evening, and we hit the road to the Little Bighorn Battlefield National Monument in southern Montana. We got to Bighorn around eight o'clock. Unfortunately the visitor center had closed, and the rangers had left. We could still walk around, and we saw the many precisely arranged headstones in the national cemetery. We walked up to Last Stand Hill, pausing to read monuments and historical markers. We gazed down at the section of the hill where headstones marked spots where many of the soldiers fell during the battle, including the one with General Custer's name on it. We also stopped at the Indian memorial, a really cool iron sculpture on a cement platform. This was one of the places where a silver lining was pulled out of a cloud. Even though we were late and missed some of the possible activities at Bighorn, we experienced an awesome sight when the setting sun hit the horizon in the west and the moon appeared on the opposite horizon. It was a great way to end our day of touring.

07/09/2006

Little Bighorn Battlefield National Monument

Now it was on to the hotel in Billings. The hour-long trip included another unexpected experience as clouds, lightning, and storms north of us in the night sky put on a tremendous show as we drove on I-90. We got to the hotel, settled in, and hit the pool for a short dip to unwind.

Monday was here, and we checked out and hit the road. We had about three hours to get to Yellowstone National Park. Since I was still a little unsure of my driving in high places, we passed through Gardiner, Montana, and headed south toward the park on Highway 89. It was a pretty trip in a low valley along the Yellowstone River. We saw many nice ranches and farms, and the mountains of Yellowstone rose up in front of us as we approached the north entrance. *The main roads in Yellowstone are loops in the shape of an eight with five spokes leading to the different park entrances.* Soon after we entered the park, we armed ourselves with the park newspaper to augment the National Park Service brochure and other documents I had printed.

Our first stop was the Mammoth Hot Springs area. This is located at the top left of the eight. There are plenty of amenities available here. We ventured up the trails and boardwalks toward the natural beauty of this place. We marveled at the colorful mineral terraces. These are formations of rock steps with amazing colors and contours. We passed some terraces and walked the trails up toward large mineral pools. The springs gave off steam, radiated beautiful colors, and emitted strong smells that the kids noticed right away. It almost smelled as bad as the inside of our car after the burritos, but the sights were definitely worth the sulfurous odors. We got a great introduction to one of Yellowstone's natural wonders, and I recommend taking as much time as you can on the Mammoth Hot Springs trails.

07/10/2006

Yellowstone National Park — Mammoth Hot Springs

One of the events we had reserved was the early evening Old West Cookout. This was a chuck wagon ride from the Roosevelt Lodge at the top right of the eight. After we spent a few hours at Mammoth Hot Springs, we drove over to the Roosevelt Lodge. We had some time before the dinner, so we drove up the road a little way and took a trail down to the river. We were actually pretty high up, and the trail was a fairly strenuous one to get down to the water. We saw some wildlife, alive and not, and we headed back to the lodge after we climbed back up. While we were waiting for the cookout, it rained for a short time. It was not much, and amazingly, because of the extremely low humidity in Yellowstone, we were dry soon after it stopped. We gathered in the waiting area with scores of other cookout-goers, and we loaded up in our horse-drawn wagons. The trip took us through a valley and meadows to a camp where the cowboys and park workers were preparing everything. There were storytelling, a sing-along, a campfire, some wildlife, and general wandering around. Steaks were prepared on a huge grill, and we enjoyed vegetables, salads, and fruit. It was an experience worth the effort. When we got back, it was time to drive to our room at Grant Village near the bottom right of the eight. It was dusk, and it turns out that part of this route included switchbacks at high altitudes with no guardrails. It was not too bad, but I did become edgy and navigated slower than usual. The last part of the drive went around Lake Yellowstone, and we saw some of the forest that had been scorched back in 1988. We made it to Grant Village, and we settled into our room in an apartment-like setting. Grant Village has a convenient visitor/administration center, a general store with lots of choices, and some very nice restaurants. It did not have the rustic grandeur of the Lake Yellowstone Lodge or the Old Faithful Inn; however, the rooms were nice, and the location was well maintained. Our next adventure was coming Tuesday morning, so we fell asleep quickly.

Since we were new to the park, I thought a guided tour would ensure that we see many of the main attractions of Yellowstone. Research and self-guided tours are good, but it helps to have someone knowledgeable pointing out certain aspects of the land. I had booked the "Circle of Fire" daylong bus tour for Tuesday. The bus picked us up right at the Grant Village visitor center, so we did not have to scramble in the morning. This tour takes you around the lower circle of the eight, where the majority of the famous features of the park are located. The driver was our guide, narrating the trip and informing us of important features and places. We stopped at Yellowstone Lake, Hayden Valley, the Upper and Lower Falls of the Grand Canyon of the Yellowstone, and the Fountain Paint Pot Nature Trail. There were also stops for wildlife. The guide can be adamant about protocols in the park, and ours yelled at a number of people who got way too close to animals while they were trying to get pictures of them. We also stopped for lunch and enjoyed a tourist area where we ate at a lunch counter and watched funny videos of what happens when people get too close to the animals. I guess the guide was right. The final destination late in the afternoon was Old Faithful so that we could witness one of its consistent eruptions.

As with any tour like this one, you see a lot, but you are on a schedule, so excessive meandering is not a luxury you have. It does, however, give you a good feel for the major hot spots and the ones you might like to come back to and spend some more time exploring. You also learn things about the lodgepole pine trees, the volcanoes under the park, the natural wonders in the park, the wildlife, and early Yellowstone pioneers. We saw mineral pools, hot springs, fumerols, steam vents, mud and paint pots, waterfalls, geysers, and a bunch of just plain awesomeness. Again we ended the tour at the Old Faithful Inn complex near the bottom left of the eight. We roamed the grounds to see other geysers, checking out the inn and gift shop and then sitting along the edge of Old Faithful for the eruption. The geyser eruption was pretty amazing, and I would recommend seeing it multiple times at different times of the day. This will give you different sky colors for a background and make for varied photographic shots. The bus then took us across the Continental Divide and back to Grant Village. We disembarked, went to our room, got cleaned up, and then headed right back to the Old Faithful Inn for dinner. The great room is lit by natural light and also candlelight, so it takes you back in time. The dining room was quite nice, and the food was worth the experience. After dinner we headed back to Grant Village to retire for the night. We had another busy day ahead of us.

07/11/2006

Yellowstone National Park — Old Faithful

Wednesday brought two more paid excursions, and the first one was in the morning. It was the "Saddle Up" partial day horse tour. This took place in the Canyon Village area of the park at the middle right of the eight. The four of us each got on a horse along with about a dozen other riders and the guides. This was a pretty mild ride. We stayed in a continuous line so any predators did not sense a break where they could attack. We rode through meadows and wooded areas at a relatively slow pace, enjoying the scenery. The whole tour took several hours. It did not get too crazy, but the kids loved the horses nonetheless. Small adventures like this can help to mitigate the pain the kids might feel when they have to do more hiking. However, if they enjoy extensive hiking, then you are golden. Fortunately we had some time between the horse ride and our next adventure, and one of the spots we made it a point to return to from the Tuesday bus ride was the Grand Canyon of the Yellowstone and the Lower Falls. This was close to the stable area, so it gave us a convenient opportunity to see the falls again. We hiked along ridge trails high above the river, and we got some excellent views of a spectacular waterfall and the canyon river it feeds. This is one of the highlights of the park among the many other natural wonders.

Yellowstone National Park — Lower Falls

After noon we also had a reservation for a guided fishing tour on a boat on Lake Yellowstone. This was to only be a few hours. My kids enjoy fishing and the water, and I wanted to relax and let someone else do the driving. The Bridge Bay Marina is on the same side of the road system about halfway back to Grant Village from the Canyon area, so we were in good shape. We got to the docks and checked in, and we had some time to peruse the gift shop and buy supplies and sweatshirts. Lake Yellowstone is large and beautiful, and our captain took us out toward where we hoped the fish were. The morning was kind of overcast and white with spotty sunshine. By the time we hit the middle of the lake, it was totally overcast. That does not bother the fishermen, but what we experienced does. Over the lake off to the east definite storm clouds had formed, and we could see the rain coming down in the distance. I still wanted to fish, but the captain mentioned something about capsizing, so we had to go back in. The red flags were up all over, so the storm was going to hit us. We were a little disappointed that we did not get to fish. However, there was another silver lining out of actual clouds. We enjoyed a nice boat ride on Lake Yellowstone, and they refunded our money because of the weather cancellation. All things considered, I would have preferred to fish, but it worked out given the circumstances. We did have a conversation with some of the fishermen at the dock, and they asked us about our trip. We told them we were going to Zion next, and one of them replied that Zion was his favorite park. We were hoping his recommendation would affirm our choice.

We left the docks and headed south back to Grant Village. We did take some time to stop and wander around the Lake Yellowstone Hotel. Like the Old Faithful Inn, this is a stop worth the time. On our way back to the room we pulled off the road at a turnout and watched the rain hit the lake. We relaxed and enjoyed yet another beautiful nature show. We had a very long drive on Thursday, so getting back to the room and relaxing was appealing to all of us. We also had reservations at the Grant Village Lake House restaurant that evening, and the view and the food turned out to provide an enjoyable experience.

In addition to food, liquid refreshments are something you want to think about when you are visiting the park. Of course, it is important to have plenty of water available. Any other drinks, such as juice, milk, soda pop, and sport drinks, are available to help keep you hydrated. I always like to sample local beers. Fortunately in the Yellowstone area the Grand Teton Brewing Company is billed as the original brewery of Yellowstone and the Grand Teton national parks. The Grant Village general store as well as the restaurants where we dined had their beers available. My two favorites on this trip were the Old Faithful Ale and Bitch Creek ESB. (Yes, that is the actual name.) Both are very tasty, and I hope to get back there to enjoy them again.

As I close the book on the Yellowstone part of this odyssey, I want to mention that another enjoyable characteristic of the park is the abundance of wildlife. There are better times to see more of it than the hottest time of the year, but we did see our share of bison, deer, pronghorns, foxes, elk, and one wolf, I think. We did not venture too far off the beaten paths where we would likely have encountered even more varieties, so that is a goal of mine when I eventually return. I would definitely like to see bears in some of their awesome natural habitats. Just make sure not to get too close, or you might get yelled at or become the subject of a funny but serious video.

Thursday was the big driving day. The trip down from Yellowstone in northwest Wyoming to Zion in southwest Utah was approximately seven hundred miles, and only half was on the flat and straight I-15. This would be a day of many sights, stories, and memories, almost all of which were enjoyable. The highlights will offer even more reasons to want to come here. I got up before sunrise Thursday morning and took a quick walk through the woods to Yellowstone Lake to see the sunrise and the calm water. I took some pictures and enjoyed the serenity before we embarked on the long drive to Zion. One advantage of staying in Grant Village was being just up the road from the south entrance of the park. We checked out, picked up some supplies, and headed down Highway 89. I was counting on some beautiful scenery along the way, and I was not disappointed. We passed some smaller lakes, pretty meadows, and wooded areas, stopping briefly at a waterfall to take a few pictures. We also stopped at the park entrance/exit to take our pictures with the park sign. Shortly after we left Yellowstone, we entered the area of another gorgeous location in Big Sky Country. This was Grand Teton National Park. While we had no time to really explore it, just being able to drive past the snowcapped mountains and the valleys of wildflowers gave us something awesome to look at. However, the curvy two-lane highway did present a little inconvenience. A car pulling a motor home was in front of us and going about forty for what seemed like an eternity. You seem to remember things like this, but at least we could enjoy the mountains as we crawled along. I definitely want to get back to the Tetons to do some hiking and fishing, maybe in Phelps Lake. This lake is located near the entrance to Death Canyon. That name seems appropriate. Our first stop of the day was a quick pit stop in Jackson Hole. This is a very nice resort town, and I recommend more time here; however, we were just passing through. We also passed through Afton, another pretty western Wyoming town.

As Highway 89 crossed into Idaho for a brief time, we encountered yet another beautiful place that I would love to return to. Bear Lake is a huge turquoise lake that straddles Idaho and Utah, and it seems to go on forever. One negative about this place at that particular time was that we got stuck in construction traffic. Fortunately it only delayed us about a half hour, and we did get to enjoy the aquatic scenery for a longer period of time. Shortly after we entered Utah, Highway 89 veered southwest toward Logan, mountains, and Interstate 15. Yet again we were delayed a couple of times by a rock slide and a herd of mountain goats. Fortunately these were not too time-consuming. We stopped for lunch and a break in Logan, Utah, and then started on the last leg toward I-15. During all of this we discovered another silver lining of sorts in a fast-food meal toy. In 2006, Captain Jack Sparrow was still popular, and the boys got Captain Jack dolls with one of their meals. Since this was before the boys had purchased MP3 players and headphones for themselves, they could not just tune out during the ride. Somehow the dolls were a source of entertainment that kept them happy and laughing the whole day. Thank you, thank you, thank you.

We finally hit I-15 around two o'clock in the afternoon, and we still had approximately 350 miles still to go to get to Zion. Luckily I-15 allowed us to go fast. We hit a little traffic going through Salt Lake City, but we made excellent time. We exited onto Highways 17 and then 9 near dusk, and we made our way toward the entrance of the park. As soon as you get to the edge of the park, you see the incredible Navajo

Sandstone mountain faces and rock formations. The colors are amazing, and your excitement grows. Since we were staying in the park at the Zion Lodge, we already had our pass to drive into the park. The road into the park has mountains on one side and the Virgin River on the other. It is a fantastic sight. Our room was in one of the apartment-like outbuildings near the main lodge, and we were right at the base of a mountain. We quickly checked in and unloaded, heading over to dinner at the Red Rock Grill just after eight o'clock. The food was good, and I was savoring my fish; however, this is where we would learn another life lesson. Do not let your young child drink a carbonated cola drink and then a glass of chocolate milk before you have any food. The chemical reaction in his stomach made him sick, so I had to rush him into the bathroom. He finally expelled it, and we went back. My fish had cooled off, but it was still very good. He did get something to eat, so we were good to go. We wandered around a little and then retired to our room. The accommodations were very nice and well worth the price.

The next morning we knew we only had until noon, so we ate and did some hiking around the lodge and the emerald pools after we picked up the park newspaper. Around midmorning we took the shuttle bus up toward the Temple of Sinawava, where the pavement ends and the Narrows begin. We stopped at the shuttle drop-off and walked the trail toward the water. Many people walking the other way were soaked, so we knew we were close to the Virgin River and the Narrows. When we got there, we did not have enough time to explore too far, so we waded into the water for a short period of time. Along the shuttle route on the way back, we also stopped at Weeping Rock. A short trail takes you to a spot where the water has made its way through the sandstone and is finally spitting out the side of the mountain. There are cool, covered areas where mosses and plants are growing because of the water, even as the outside temperature approaches triple digits. This was a relaxing and beautiful respite. The shuttle trip was not long, taking us through picturesque areas of trees and colorful mountains. I took many pictures to capture the contrasting colors. We got dropped off near the Grotto, hiked back to the lodge, and eventually checked out. As we left, I knew that one morning was not nearly enough for this place, so it, too, was added to the list of my future return destinations. The fisherman at Yellowstone was right about this place.

07/14/2006

Zion National Park

Well, we were now on our last leg of the trip. It was Friday around noon, and we had about a three-hour drive to Las Vegas. While much of this drive was through desert, we were in for a pleasant surprise as we briefly drove through the beautiful mountains in the northwest tip of Arizona. We were only in Arizona for a short time between Utah and Nevada, but the scenery was stunning. You wind through rock face after rock face, and then all of a sudden you are in the clear and passing into Nevada. This is where the heat makes itself known. At one point on the way to Las Vegas, the car thermometer registered 116 degrees, and it was near 110 when we got to the Excalibur hotel. Our friends were meeting us Saturday, so we had Friday afternoon to enjoy at the pool. To cap off the trip, I had reserved two shows for us to see. The Friday night show was the Blue Man Group show at the Venetian hotel. We had seen them at smaller venues in New York City and Chicago a few years before this trip, and I wanted the boys and my wife to see the really big Vegas show. We had seats about fifteen rows from the stage, and it did not disappoint. We met the performers after the show, and the boys had a great time. We also introduced them to something new as we hit the Las Vegas Strip on a hot summer night. We walked out of the Venetian around ten o'clock, and it was still nearly 100 degrees. There were people everywhere, and the lights and activity gave the boys a memorable experience for all of their senses.

Our friends arrived Saturday, and we spent the day wandering around the places near the Excalibur and playing at the pool. We enjoyed one more added bonus on Saturday. I have a cousin who lives in Las Vegas, and we were able to spend time with her and her family. It is an added benefit when you can travel far away, enjoy the scenery, and see friends and family you would otherwise rarely see. We then prepared for the King Arthur's Tournament and Joust show. The large amphitheater under the Excalibur is filled with sand, and we had a medieval dinner and cheered during the games and the battle. The eight-thirty show was rousing fun for the kids and us parents, and it was a great way to put an exclamation point on a fabulous family trip. We cheered wildly for our knight, booed the other knights, and enjoyed the medieval fare and serving wenches. Afterward we stopped for ice cream and eventually went to bed.

Sunday morning was pretty leisurely, as we did not have to be at the airport too early. We had breakfast and then went to the airport, bidding our friends farewell. The flight home was uneventful, and after we drove from the Pittsburgh airport, we were home Sunday night. It was kind of a bittersweet day. It is always nice to get home, but the best trip ever was over. Fortunately I had accumulated many ideas for the sequel.

SUMMATION

Well, there you have it—*a weeklong vacation out West to the Badlands National Park, Mount Rushmore National Memorial, Devils Tower National Monument, Little Bighorn Battlefield National Monument, Yellowstone National Park, the Grand Tetons National Park, Zion National Park, and Las Vegas!* Wow! It was fun, inspiring, informative, beautiful, and memorable. I learned more about proper planning, and I learned more about many of the fantastic places we can visit in our country. I also learned that after the determination of how to get there (air, rail, bus, car, RV, wagon train, etc.), this trip can be done at a relatively low cost. I added tours, dinners, lodging, etc., but the main focus of exploring the parks and monuments can be done inexpensively. I cannot guarantee that every place we visited back in 2006 is as good as it was then. You will have to do that research. What does endure, however, is the magnificence of the national parks and national monuments, and they are there for you to enjoy.

Again there are uncounted sources of information on these places. The research is a huge part of the fun you can have when you are planning and taking a trip like this. I have chronicled the steps we took and the experiences we enjoyed during the process of taking the best trip ever. Armed with this knowledge, you can set out to research, plan, and experience some truly fantastic locations. If you can manage to take more than a week and can afford the cost, you can expand your options, including more time at each park, renting an RV (Cruise America, El Monte, etc.), and even making stops at some of the places we originally bypassed.

07/14/2006

Family at Weeping Rock in Zion National Park

I am glad I can say we actually visited these places, but I found out that we only scratched the surface of what we could see and do. Nevertheless, I highly recommend this trip in its original incarnation or in some modified version. You will not be disappointed. It will inspire you and make you want to see even more. That is what it did for me.

CHAPTER 2: WESTERN ODYSSEY #2
THE GRAND CANYON (2008)

PREPARATIONS

The 2006 vacation was so much fun that I knew we had to go back out west. While I wanted to go as soon as possible, I wanted to accrue enough miles on my credit card to be able to obtain airline tickets for no cost. This meant waiting until 2008. It did not mean that I had to wait to start planning. I fell in love with Utah, even though we were only there for about a day in 2006. Thus, I wanted to return there. Furthermore, to follow up our visit to America's first national park, I thought it fitting to visit the Grand Canyon. This natural wonder is only a few hours from southern Utah, so it would be a perfect centerpiece to our second big vacation adventure. This would also give us the opportunity to meet our friends from California and spend another few days with them in Arizona and Las Vegas. Believe it or not, we also have other friends. A friend and former colleague of my wife lives in a suburb of Denver, so the trip's beginning and ending points were coalescing in my mind. Extensive online research and mapping allowed me to pick places and times within the constraints I had to work under.

Step one was choosing when we would go. July again turned out to work the best for us. The boys' summer schedules can be as hectic as their school-year schedules, so midsummer works well. It is generally very warm in July in Colorado, Utah, Arizona, and Nevada, but some of the elevations we experienced were quite comfortable. Plus, the dryness made the higher temperatures more bearable.

Step two was figuring out how we would get there from Pennsylvania. My plan to build credit card airline miles was progressing, and we would have enough miles by early 2008 to obtain the tickets for no cost, aside from the standard security charges. However, one of the pitfalls of this approach would befall us. There are some limitations to using miles to purchase tickets. Since we were flying into Denver and flying home from Las Vegas, the flight itinerary was somewhat unconventional. The availability of return flights ended up cutting our available vacation time short by one day. We had to fly back Saturday instead of Sunday, and we actually had to split the flights. Two of us flew home early in the morning, and the other two flew home on a separate flight in the afternoon. It turned out to be a minor inconvenience, but we still saved a few thousand dollars over the posted fares.

Step three was determining where we were going to visit and on what days. We knew we were staying with friends in Denver on Saturday and that it would take several days to get to the Grand Canyon. The original plan was to stay Wednesday, Thursday, and Friday nights (July 16–18) at the Grand Canyon. Knowing the popularity of the park, I made the lodging reservations almost a year ahead of time in September 2007. This was the cornerstone of the trip, and I would build around it. Because of the flight changes, we would have to cancel Friday night at the Canyon. In between Colorado and Arizona is Utah, and this was to provide the second major piece of the adventure. Arches National Park and Canyonlands National Park are located near Moab, Utah. In southwestern Utah, there is Bryce Canyon National Park. These were the targets for the first half of the week. So the trip route was set— Denver with friends on Saturday, a beautiful drive through Colorado, the Colorado National Monument, and eastern Utah on Sunday, Moab and the Arches National Park on Monday, Canyonlands and a scenic drive through Capitol Reef National Park and Grand Staircase Escalante National Monument on Tuesday, Bryce Canyon National Park on Tuesday evening and Wednesday morning, the Grand Canyon National Park North Rim on Wednesday and Thursday, rafting in the

Glen Canyon National Recreation Area on Thursday, and Las Vegas on Friday evening! This was going to be the second best trip ever!

Step four was determining where we were going to stay. Saturday was set as we were staying with friends in a Denver suburb. I like to stay inside the national parks, but Arches does not have any in-park lodging. I then looked for the nicest lodging near the park, and I found the Sorrel River Ranch on a scenic highway outside of Moab. I encourage you to check out their website and offerings because it is not inexpensive to stay there. It is, however, definitely worth the money if you can fit it into your budget. After two nights at Sorrel River Ranch, our next stop would be the Bryce Canyon Lodge inside the park. We reserved a western cabin five months before the trip. We decided to stay at the North Rim of the Grand Canyon, and the lodge has a variety of cabins to choose from. Because of the flight schedule change, we ended up having to stay in two different cabins at the North Rim.

Step five was adding tours and additional activities on to the location visits. I wanted to get a little more adventurous with the hiking since the boys were older, so I searched for excursions in the Moab area. After some online research I found the Moab Adventure Center. They have a half-day canyoneering trip, so this would be a physical adventure the boys and the adults would enjoy. I also reserved the Fiery Furnace tour inside the Arches. I then chose a raft trip on the Colorado River that originated in Page, Arizona. Everything else would be self-led and ad hoc.

Step six was choosing certain meals to get a little fancy with. The first big meal was chosen by our Denver hosts the first night, and the restaurant of choice was Casa Bonita. We also reserved dinners at the Bryce Canyon Lodge and the Grand Canyon North Rim Lodge. Each place has a very nice restaurant.

Step seven was choosing what vehicle we would drive around in. We chose a midsize all-wheel-drive vehicle. Again we would be dropping the vehicle off at a different location from where we picked it up, so it would be more expensive regardless of the vehicle we chose.

Step eight was making sure we had the right supplies. Clothing, eyewear, electronics, cameras, snacks, and other related travel gear were prepped based on our experiences and preferences. As always, the hiking shoes are important, and my wife and I still had our Merrells from 2006.

The boys' feet had continued to grow, so they needed different shoes. They found comfortable shoes for active use with soles that gripped. I did upgrade my video camera to a higher quality unit with a hard drive and multiple batteries. I also took the older tape-based camera as well as multiple digital cameras with increasing megapixels.

Step nine was budgeting for the Great Western Odyssey #2. The worksheet below is also taken from of the spreadsheet file I have used for all of our major trips. It shows the plans for the schedule, locations, activities, estimated costs and miles, and the timing of the payments for each item. Actual costs were added for improved accuracy. My goal again was to spread out the costs over time as much as possible.

			2008 TRAVEL COSTS FOR OUR FUN					
DATES	DESTINATION	ITEM	COST ESTIMATE	PREPAID	DATES	MILES	ACTUAL
07/08	Western swing II	Flights — add'l costs	100.00	100.00	2/20/2008		100.00
07/08	Western swing II	Casa Bonita Dinner (07/12)	90.00		7/12/2008	50	0.00
07/08	Western swing II	Sorrel River Night 1 (07/13)	500.31	500.31	2/16/2008	360	500.31
07/08	Western swing II	Sorrel River Night 1 Dinner (07/13) 7:00 p.m.	100.00		7/13/2008		175.00
07/08	Western swing II	Tracy — Massage (07/13)	100.00		7/13/2008		127.20
07/08	Western swing II	Tours — Ephedra's Grotto (07/14) 7:15 a.m.	366.00		7/14/2008		394.56
07/08	Western swing II	Tours — Fiery Furnace (07/14) 4:00 p.m.	50.00		7/14/2008	60	0.00
07/08	Western swing II	Sorrel River Night 2 (07/14)	500.31	500.31	6/13/2008		500.31
07/08	Western swing II	Sorrel River Night 2 Dinner (07/14)	100.00		7/13/2008		63.00
07/08	Western swing II	Bryce Canyon Lodging (07/15)	183.40	183.40	2/25/2008	275	183.40
07/08	Western swing II	Bryce Canyon Dinner (07/15) 7:00 p.m.	90.00		7/15/2008		120.00
07/08	Western swing II	Grand Canyon 1st Night (07/16)	119.48	119.48	9/15/2007	160	119.48
07/08	Western swing II	Grand Canyon 1st Night Dinner (07/16)	90.00		7/16/2008		0.00
07/08	Western swing II	Tours — Canyon Rafting (07/17) 7:00 a.m.-12:30	294.00	294.00	6/21/2008	250	294.00
07/08	Western swing II	Grand Canyon 2nd Night Dinner (07/17)	90.00		7/17/2008		216.65
07/08	Western swing II	Grand Canyon 2nd Night (07/17)	130.00		7/18/2008		154.55
07/08	Western swing II	Tours — Grand Canyon (07/18) ????			Did Not Happen		0.00

| | | 2008 TRAVEL COSTS FOR OUR FUN | | | | | |
DATES	DESTINATION	ITEM	COST ESTIMATE	PREPAID	DATES	MILES	ACTUAL
07/08	Western swing II	Grand Canyon 3rd Night Dinner (07/18)	50.00		7/18/2008		0.00
07/08	Western swing II	Leave the night of the 18th for Vegas				280	
07/08	Western swing II	Car Rental 07/12/08-07/19/08	566.83		7/19/2008		653.03
07/08	Western swing II						
07/08	Western swing II	Park Fees — Estimates	125.00		07/08		0.00
07/08	Western swing II	Meals estimate 07/13-07/18 (est. $50/day)	300.00		07/08		122.97
07/08	Western swing II	Misc. Food			07/08		88.82
07/08	Western swing II	Misc., Nick Knacks	150.00		07/08		101.09
07/08	Western swing II	Gas (estimate 25 mpg x $4 x Tot Miles)	229.60		07/08		343.55
07/08	Western swing II						
07/08	Western swing II	Cash — Initial	300.00				300.00
07/08	Western swing II	Cash — ATM's on trip	201.75				201.75
07/08	Western swing II	Parking — Airport 07/19/08 (Pd. Cash from above)	0.00				
July	2,560.42	Totals	$4,826.68	1,697.50		1,435	4,759.67
Pre-	1,697.50				Actual	1,680	
Cash	501.75						
	4,759.67						

THE TRIP!

The excitement kept building, and now it was July 2008. Our flight out of Pittsburgh was early morning on Saturday the twelfth. Taking advantage of the time change, we arrived in Denver with plenty of sunlight left in the day. The flights were uneventful, and we picked up our luggage and chose a Ford Edge as our trip mobile. Our friends were in a suburb on the west side of Denver, so we took I-70 from the airport through Denver to their house. We relaxed, visited, and prepared for our dinner at Casa Bonita. This is a very popular Mexican restaurant in the Denver area, and it is billed as a restaurant and family entertainment destination. The food was very good (though my favorite is still Herrera's in Dallas), and the atmosphere was quite festive. There was a waterfall with cliff divers, stage shows, bands, a gift shop, and an arcade. We enjoyed the festivities and the food to close out our first day of the trip. We went back to our friend's house with the intent of more relaxing and visiting. I, on the other hand, had made the mistake of pulling an all-nighter at work the night before, so I fell asleep soon after we got back. I am sure everyone else enjoyed it.

Sunday morning arrived, and we said farewell to our friends. We were close to I-70, and that was the main road for the day. Denver is on the edge of the Rocky Mountains National Park, and we had to pass through the park and a number of national forests to get across the state. The drive was very enjoyable and picturesque, particularly without the threat of snow. We passed through tunnels, mountains, forests, lakes, rivers, and ski resorts. One well-known ski resort town is Vail, and we enjoyed the view as we drove through it. We had about 250 miles from Denver to Utah, and shortly before the border we stopped in Grand Junction, Colorado. I had done a little research, and I found out there is a really nice rock/mountain/canyon location near Grand Junction called the Colorado National Monument. You can hike, camp, watch the sunrise, bicycle, and climb rocks there. We did not do any of those things. We did, however, take the twenty-three-mile historic Rim Rock Drive around the park. We drove through tunnels, stopped at scenic overlooks, did some mild walking to marked spots, and relaxed in the sun for a short time.

Colorado National Monument

We enjoyed the canyons and the colorful sandstone, and we saw some wildlife. It was a nice way to break up the day and get a feel for what we would be enjoying in Utah. After our tour we were on our way again. We continued along I-70 and the Colorado River, and soon we were in Utah. Now it was going to get even more interesting.

About a half hour into Utah on I-70, we exited on Business Route 6 to Highway 128. We were soon driving along the Colorado River, and we stopped briefly to stretch our legs and take some pictures along the river. We started seeing more mesas protruding high out of the ground, and the deep reddish orange color of the dirt and rocks was becoming more intense. Highway 128 is a beautiful drive, and there are many trail roads intersecting it. We stayed on the road for a while, and we eventually arrived at the Sorrel River Ranch around midafternoon. This resort and spa is advertised as the place where "luxury meets adventure" in the Moab area. Again this is not an inexpensive place to stay, but it turned out to be very memorable and fun. There are more resorts and ranches along Highway 128, and there are plenty of other places to stay in the Moab area. We had reserved two nights at Sorrel River in February. The main gate was almost a half mile from the lodge and cabins, so we drove the distance and were met by friendly staff. We checked in and unloaded our stuff into an excellent two level cabin that had all the amenities we needed and a beautiful view of the Colorado River and the bluffs beyond. We did not have anything specific planned for the afternoon, but we did make reservations at 7:00 p.m. for a buffet dinner on the River Deck next to the Colorado. We were able to check out the horse stables, the tennis courts, the pool, and other activities. For a gift I bought my wife a massage at the spa, and she totally enjoyed it. Guys, I recommend this, as it was money well spent. The views from Sorrel River are spectacular in all directions, and it is very peaceful. We enjoyed the outdoor dinner, played some games, and relaxed for the night. Monday was going to be busy.

I had found the Moab Adventure Center while I was researching things to do around the Moab area. They partner with a number of other organizations to offer park tours, off-road excursions, water trips, horseback and slick-rock bike riding, and canyoneering among other things. I wanted a hiking experience that was interesting and challenging, something that would be a new experience for my wife and the boys. The "Ephedra's Grotto" canyoneering trip looked like the perfect introduction. The five-hour adventure offered a scenic, informative, and physically engaged experience. We chose the morning session, so we had to be at the center by 7:00 a.m. This provided us with a pleasant surprise. The morning ride along Highway 128 into Moab was gorgeous. As the sun was creeping up, we wound around the Colorado River and the rock faces, trees, cliffs, animals, and the valley below for about seventeen miles. The cool thing about this was we would have to drive it again several times, further enjoying the beauty of it. The road ends at Highway 191, where Moab is just to the south, and Arches is shortly up the road to the northwest.

At the center we prepped our clothes, met the guide, and packed the supplies and equipment we would need for the hike. Water and granola bars were very important here. There was a short drive to the starting point just outside Moab, and we were left in the slick rock wilderness with our guide. The terrain included sand, bushes, sloped slick rock, trees, streams, washes, hills, canyons, rock faces, and stone bridges.

Early on, as we were making our way into the hills, we had to meet the first fitness test. We had to jump across a ravine from one rock to another. The large rocks sloped down toward one another, creating a crevasse, so we were not just jumping from one ledge to another. The guide told us to jump and run. As soon as we hit the rock on the other side, we had to pump our legs and run up the side of the slick, sloped rock face. With proper hiking shoes, it was not extremely difficult. However, my wife had recently had knee surgery, so this would be a test of how well she could support herself in a physical situation like this. Fortunately she passed the test with flying colors, as did the boys and I. We continued our trek, and the guide would explain some of the history and geology of the area we were exploring. After a while we got to the first rappel site. We looked down into a hole about a hundred feet down. Halfway down there was a ledge that we had to climb over to finish the rope drop. The guide fitted us with helmets, harnesses, and carabiners. These metal rings with clasps were used to allow a slow and controlled descent. There were connectors in the rock faces that he used to secure the ropes and release mechanisms. He told us stories of rappelling mishaps, but he assured us everything would be fine. I had rappelled in college, and I pretty much knew what to expect, so I went first. This rappel was all facing a rock structure, so we could use our legs to walk ourselves down to the first ledge and the bottom. We ended up surrounded by stone walls. Everyone made it without any issues, and we continued our hike in the sand below.

Not long after the first descent we came to a large natural stone bridge. One hundred and twenty feet below it was a green canyon with sand and water sources. The top of the bridge where we would rappel from was about thirty feet thick. After that, the remaining descent was done suspended in the air. We still maintained a partially seated position as we went down, lowering ourselves one by one. My oldest son and I were the only ones to have a little trouble, but nothing major. We exited into the open, continuing to make our way up and down through trails, rocks, and plant life. Near the end of the hike, we stopped for snacks at a stream running through bushes and large rocks. My youngest son handed off his backpack and waded into the waist-high water. The sun was now high in the sky, and the water was very refreshing.

Canyoneering in Moab, Utah

It was nearing noon, and we soon came out into the open and up to a roadside turnout. There were many rocks to climb on as we waited to get picked up for the ride back to the center. We also spied nesting locations for large birds. This was our introduction to canyoneering, not just hiking, and it was a blast. After we got back to the center, we thanked our guide, and we headed for lunch. We still had more to do that day.

Originally I had reserved the "Fiery Furnace" tour for Monday afternoon in Arches National Park. This is led by a park ranger, and it is inexpensive. However, in my zeal to fill our time, it turned out to be somewhat strenuous and similar to the "Ephedra's Grotto" hike we had just finished. Therefore, I cancelled that tour, and instead we went back to Sorrel River Ranch to relax and swim in their fantastic pool. This gave us a chance to unwind and enjoy the Highway 128 scenery when we went in the other direction. We still were going to go tour Arches, but it would be self-led and leisurely later that afternoon. We spent some time at the pool and then regrouped and headed off for Arches. Once again we were able to take in the beauty of Highway 128 at a different time of day.

The National Park Service official Arches brochures contain a lot of useful information, and the park map is especially helpful. It also tells you to be careful not to damage any of the cryptobiotic crust on the ground. This living substance is important, and you are advised to stay on the trails and slick rock to avoid it. The visitors' center is right near the entrance of the park, and the fee is reasonable if you do not already have an annual park pass. We made sure to take a lot of water with us, though we would not be on any hike for an extended period of time. The paved park road is only about twenty miles from the park entrance to its end at the Devil's Garden trailhead, and there are many stops, trails, and paved side roads to magnificent rock attractions. Right off the bat you make some hairpin turns and noticeable elevation shifts as you make your way into the heart of the park. While we were driving through the park, we spied some places where we wanted to stop as we would make our way back from our first destination—the Delicate Arch viewpoints. The trail to the Delicate Arch is a fairly strenuous three-mile round-trip hike, so we decided to take the easy one-hundred-yard trail to the viewpoints. While we did not get to walk under the arch, we did get beautiful views of it from a distance over a large chasm. We also had fun on the easy trail, as there were offshoots and rocks to climb on and explore. We got a great feel for the size of the Delicate Arch. We saw people near it, and they looked like tiny dots compared to it. However, the pictures we took also showed how small the Delicate Arch really is relative to the land and stone around it. The Delicate Arch is essentially like a Utah state mascot, and it is prominent in literature and on license plates. Thus, like a famous general from the twentieth century, I vowed to return to the Arch itself. We then headed to the northern end of the paved park road.

We got to the Devil's Garden a short time later, and we checked out the signage near the parking area. We took the trailhead, stopping to climb rocks, check out jackrabbits and cacti, and enjoy the afternoon sun. There were many rocks and shapes along with narrow paths through the sand and brush. There were also a number of named arches in this area. We did not venture too far, as we had a number of other places to check out. Some of the trails were identified as strenuous, so we kept this stop fairly brief. We did manage to take a lot of pictures. We headed back south toward the Windows Section, stopping at a number of turnouts to gaze, walk, climb, take pictures, and relax among the many amazing rock formations. After we turned onto the road to get to the Windows, we saw the huge openings looming larger as we approached. It was late in the day, and the sun was making really cool reflections in some of the rock windows. The trail of steps to the massive South Window got our heart rates up, and we snapped pictures as we got closer and closer. Since I am not a picture-taking pro, I made do with the digital cameras I had. Always strive to use the best equipment you can afford to capture pictures and video that you will love to look at again and again. Although it got a little crowded with tourists inside the window of the arch, we had a lot of fun exploring, scaling, and climbing around it. The other side presented even more adventure. There was a drop-off with large sandstone rocks that gave the boys a perfect opportunity to climb some more. There was also a beautiful view through the window of mesas and mountains in the distance. The blue sky, white clouds, green bushes, and orange/tan/red stone gave us a colorful show of the spectacular natural wonders. As the sun continued to go down, we slowly made our way out of the park. A half day of hiking again only touched the surface of the Arches, but we got a great introduction to it on a gorgeous day. I suspect we will get back there. We had dinner at a sports-themed restaurant in Moab, and we headed back to Sorrel River Ranch via scenic Highway 128.

Arches National Park

Back at Sorrel River Ranch, we relaxed and wandered around the grounds and along the Colorado River. The boys played some tennis, and as the sun went down, we took more pictures of the orange-red mesas surrounding us. We finally retired to the cabin, again enjoying the luxuriously rustic dual-level abode for one more night. The next day we had approximately 275 miles to drive through the heart of Utah to get to Bryce Canyon National Park. We were not in a hurry to get on the road extremely early, so we took some time to enjoy Sorrel in the morning. I did laundry, and we checked out the indoor restaurant (one place where I wish we would have eaten but did not get to), the fitness center, and the horses. We took advantage of more photo ops with rocks, mesas, and the Colorado River in the background. I always tried to have a camera with me, and I managed to get an unexpected picture of a hummingbird hovering just in front of our front porch. It was really cool. One unfortunate omission from my original plan was Canyonlands National Park. This park is southwest of Moab, but we were not able to squeeze enough time in to even get a cursory visit. Thus, Canyonlands made the future return list, as if I needed more reasons to want to return here. We got on the road midmorning Tuesday, and we were in for a day full of spectacular sights. Again we had to traverse Highway 128 to Moab, and we then turned northwest on Highway 191 toward I-70 West. We were able to take in some more Navajo sandstone beauty as we passed by Arches Park one more time before we hit the open country. After about an hour on 191 and 70, we turned south onto Highway 24. This is where it got more interesting and scenic. Highway 24 takes you past many mountains, buttes, mesas, and even Goblin Valley State Park and leads into Capitol Reef National Park. Some of the drive is through desolate, rocky desert, while other times you are enjoying small towns, water, and sandstone formations. There are numerous hiking trails and places to stop in the Capitol Reef area, but this was another "just passing through but plan to come back sometime" location.

Soon we were in for another treat. Just before the town of Torrey, we turned south on Highway 12 off of Highway 24. Scenic Byway 12 is approximately 124 miles of diverse landscape, and it even has its own twenty-three-page brochure. I could have taken a different route, but Highway 12 was well worth the time. We started out driving along the eastern edge of Boulder Mountain and climbed to more than nine thousand feet. Another prevalent source of beauty in southern Utah was the Dixie National Forest. We passed in and out of it three times while on SB-12, and we reached elevations of more than eleven thousand feet. There are numerous turnouts and overlooks, and these are great places to stretch for a few minutes and enjoy the views. As we passed the town of Boulder, we headed toward the town of Escalante and the Grand Staircase-Escalante National Monument. There are tunnels, byways, and trailheads that can lead to slot canyons, waterfalls, rivers, lakes, and other natural sights. We saw multicolored bluffs, cliffs, and plateaus while we made our way through little towns like Cannonville and Tropic. If you can spare the time, any of these mini adventures would be enjoyable, particularly in the Grand Staircase region. In addition to me having to drive on roads where there were drop-offs without guardrails, there were also sections of the road where we were on plateaus with drop-offs on both sides. Needless to say, I was driving at a slightly slower pace. Driving can be a monotonous chore, but when you can venture through gorgeous places like this, it becomes another memorable part of your trip.

Our ultimate destination that day was Bryce Canyon National Park, and I wanted to arrive with several hours of daylight left. Near Bryce Canyon City, we turned south on Highway 63, which led us into the park and to our lodging for the night. We made our way to the Bryce Canyon Lodge to check in and get settled. We had reserved a cabin only a short distance from the rim of the canyon. We also had reserved dinner at the lodge dining room that evening, so we set out for a short exploration of our surroundings. We went to the rim and checked out a number of trailheads and overlooks, stopping for pictures as the sun went down. We marveled at the hoodoos that make Bryce Canyon unique. These amazing spires were everywhere, displaying different jagged shapes, heights, colors, and combinations. There were sand ridges, rocks, and trees all over the canyon, and we even saw a few critters roaming around. Being at this high an elevation, we adjusted to the thinner air, and we enjoyed the weather, as the average midsummer temperature is in the upper seventies. We had a tasty meal in the dining room, and we hit the general store before we retired to our comfortable cabin. As is always the case, I set out to try more local beers. One very good sampling I enjoyed several times was Uinta Brewing

Company's Cutthroat Pale Ale. This was another delicious western treat. We rested up, knowing that we had the next morning to hike the hoodoos.

Our trip on Wednesday to the Grand Canyon was less than two hundred miles, and we were not meeting our friends until Thursday afternoon. This gave us all morning to hit some of the Bryce Canyon trails and experience the splendor of the park. Again this place should be afforded as much time as you can spare to take it all in, but any amount of time you can spend there is time well spent. With at least eight trails of four miles or less, we chose the intermediate Navajo Loop trail. This was approximately 1.5 miles that descended quickly, and it gave us a great feel for the park features. The park brochure recommends that you hike this trail in a clockwise direction, so, of course, we went counter-clockwise. We began by taking a series of steep switchbacks to descend into a small crack between two massive walls. We climbed rocks, maneuvered the trail, and eventually came out into the clear. The boys stopped to build small rock cairns, adding to the endless sculpture piles all around us. We found tall trees growing out of the rocky trails, and the boys found fallen trees to balance on and walk across. The pink, white, and tan pastels from the night before gave way to more intense orange, yellow, and red rock reflecting the morning sun. We spent quality time on the trail, taking pictures and video. We also learned an important lesson to read and heed the signs. There was a "Caution—Unstable Rocks" sign near the Two Arches area just off the trail. Of course, my eleven-year-old son had to explore it. He lost his footing on the way down and bloodily scraped up his leg in multiple places. I think he learned his lesson, and we cleaned him up back at the cabin. The Bryce Canyon brochure lists the "top ten causes of Bryce injuries," and he made number five. It also stresses proper footwear, and we did see some tourists trying to navigate the switchbacks in clogs and sandals. Not a good idea.

07/16/2008

Bryce Canyon National Park

Overall we saw some awesome sights in the park from our vantage point near the rim. Even seeing a deer wander through the park yards away from us as we went toward the trail was a memorable experience. It was time to checkout, but we still had more of the park to see. From the lodge we drove about fifteen miles south to the end of the park road. We checked out the scenic overlook at Rainbow and Yovimpa points, and then we made our way north. We stopped at turnout after turnout, including Agua Canyon, Natural Bridge, and Sunrise Point just to name a few. I recommend stopping at all of them if you have the time. We took pictures and enjoyed the views one last time as we made our way back up toward Scenic Byway 12 on our way to the Grand Canyon. We headed west on SB-12 over to Highway 89, passing more rock formations and tunnels. Heading south, we eventually got to the town of Kanab near the border. We stopped for lunch and supplies, and we turned south on Highway 89A, which took us into Arizona.

After an hour or so we passed the town of Jacob Lake and turned south on Arizona Highway 67, the North Rim Parkway. This forty-three-mile road takes you through forests, meadows, and fields on your way to the edge of a canyon that just has to be called "Grand." We had nothing specific planned that afternoon, so we went to the lodge and checked in. The North Rim Lodge is a beautiful structure with adjacent meeting rooms, terraces, gift shops, and beverage spots. The dining room and the great room have large windows that overlook the canyon below. The lodge's website uses words like breathtaking and majestic to describe the North Rim, and it is definitely accurate.

07/17/2008

Grand Canyon National Park

It is estimated that only about 10 percent of the annual Grand Canyon visitors come to the North Rim. That is exactly why I chose it. I knew we would be missing out on some South Rim vistas, but the relative solitude was worth it to me. Because of the changes we had to make to our original reservation, we stayed in two different cabins, checking out of the smaller one after the first night. This was not a big deal, except for the fact that we had reserved a boat trip in Page, Arizona, for the next morning and had to get up early. We unloaded and headed to the lodge to do some exploring. Outside of the lodge are terraces where you can relax and enjoy the view across to the South Rim with a cold drink. We ventured below the lodge on the trails, taking the Bright Angel Point Trail to get more views of the canyon and do some rock climbing. There are several other North Rim trails; however, they are five to ten miles long, and we were not ready to tackle any of these. You can also walk through the woods near the lodge along the rim of the canyon. We took plenty of pictures and eventually retired to the cabin.

The smaller cabin of the first night was connected to a room being used by another party. Shortly after midnight our anonymous connector guests arrived noisily. A couple of loud females were not able to keep quiet, so we were awakened prematurely. They finally settled down before I was forced to take action, and we managed to get some sleep. This was short-lived. We had to be at the Colorado River Discovery headquarters in Page, Arizona, by 7:00 a.m. I wanted to get the family into the water at some point, and since we did not have enough time to raft in the Grand Canyon, I chose this tour. Page is approximately 120 miles away up the North Rim Parkway and across winding sections of Highway 89. This meant we had to get up just after three in the morning and get on the road to make sure we were not late. We also had to pack everything into the car because we would not be back by eleven to officially check out of that cabin. The drive up the North Rim Parkway was actually stimulating at three thirty because it was really dark and there were animals all over the place. We had to be very vigilant so as not to hit any. The section of the trip on Highway 89 was fun, winding through barren rock and sandstone hills as the sun was peaking up in the east.

Fortunately we got to Page by seven, and we prepped for the half-day smooth-water motorized pontoon ride. A bus took the riders to the Glen Canyon dam, and we went through a dark, two-mile access tunnel before homeland security searched the bus. The tunnel was really cool.

I found out I was supposed to take my hat with me instead of trying to save my seat. Homeland Security found it and immediately questioned the group about it. Fortunately they did not arrest me, but I did get a somewhat stern talking-to. We entered the dam site and descended some seven hundred feet to our boats where the guides were waiting. The trip was approximately fifteen miles down to Lees Ferry before the actual rapids begin on the Colorado River. The water comes out of the dam at a constant 47 degrees, and in the early morning we were in the cool shadows because of the massive sandstone walls surrounding us. Drinks were available on the boat, and we were allowed to bring snacks. As the morning progressed, we popped out into the open, and the sun provided us with a spectacular day. They also run the float trips in the rain, but we enjoyed a picture-perfect day. Halfway through the float we stopped at a small beach where there were restrooms, small animals, and petroglyph wall drawings left by ancestral Puebloan people. We were also able to take a dip in the refreshing water, drying quickly in the hot sun. The voyage was a continuously winding ride through clear water and spectacular canyons, and we took picture after picture.

07/17/2008

Glen Canyon Rafting on Colorado
River near Page, Arizona

One near calamity occurred after we left the pit stop. My wife described the situation as "drinking too much soda pop" and was overcome with a personal need, but there were no facilities on the boat. She was making plans to do what needed to be done; however, the docks thankfully came into view, and the restrooms were just beyond. She raced off before we were even moored. I tipped our guide, and we boarded the bus to head back to Page. This was a relaxing ride through the desert, and it rained for a while. It was monsoon season after all. We went through mountains and canyons, crossing the Colorado on a large bridge high above the incredible river canyon below. We got back to Page just after noon, and we grabbed lunch and headed back to the North Rim. Our friends were arriving that afternoon, so we wanted to get in some hiking and fun with them before nightfall. This rafting trip did technically take away time from the Grand Canyon, but it was a fun and memorable experience that I recommend. The Page area offers a lot to do, and I hoped to return here in the future for more fun.

We checked back in Thursday afternoon, and our new cabin was a stand-alone unit that was larger than the first. We met up with our friends, and we checked out the trails near the North Rim Lodge after we downed some refreshments. We walked, talked, climbed, and snapped pictures to record our time together at the North Rim. We talked about taking a mule trip to the canyon floor, but it turns out a couple of us were just beyond the weight limit. That convenient excuse forced us to stay topside. We had reservations for eight at the lodge dining room that evening, and the meal and view were excellent. After dinner the kids played, and we did more exploring. After it got dark, we stargazed on the terrace next to the lodge. We had a great time in front of one of the most amazing backdrops in the world. We eventually retired for the night, looking forward to our last official day of the trip.

Friday morning we checked out of the lodge and headed for some of the turnouts and viewpoints around the North Rim. We spent several hours checking out different walkways and fenced-in viewing areas on the northern side of the Grand Canyon. The roads were paved but narrow, so we had to be keenly aware of other vehicles. After we enjoyed the views of the canyon walls and the Colorado River, we headed for Las Vegas. We had more than 250 miles to go to get to our friends' mother's condo. Fortunately our route took us through the northwest tip of Arizona and the beautiful mountains there. Friday night was uneventful. The kids swam. We ate pizza, and we got ready for the split flights on Saturday. Because of the awards miles limitations, my wife and oldest son flew out early in the morning, and my younger son and I flew out after noon. It was nice to get home on Saturday, as it gave us Sunday to totally unwind. Of course, it was bittersweet again, as we had to leave the beauty of the West and head back to work.

SUMMATION

So the Western Odyssey #2 was in the books. *We loved the weeklong vacation out west to Denver and the Colorado National Monument, Moab canyoneering and the Arches National Park, Scenic Byway 12 in Central Utah (including brief stops in Capitol Reef National Park and Grand Staircase-Escalante National Monument), Bryce Canyon National Park, the Grand Canyon National Park, rafting the Colorado River in Glen Canyon, and a relaxing night in Las Vegas!* We had to alter our trip in some ways, and it would have been nice to spend more time at all of the locations, but we brought back many lasting memories and a renewed admiration for the West. If you have friends in Denver and California and want to see awesome places in between, this is a trip you will love. Or if you just want to go to Arizona and Utah, the places we experienced in 2008 would be very enjoyable. Another fun discovery after the trip was seeing and hearing the results of allowing the boys to use the cameras unsupervised. Minor censoring was required. Regarding the Grand Canyon, we did not have time to ride mules, hike the floor, raft the Colorado, or check out the South Rim. Obviously these are all recommended if you have the time. However, I can say that even though our first stay there was relatively brief, "We came, we saw, and we loved it!"

Family at the Grand Canyon National Park Entrance

These are all places I want to return to, and if you have been to any of them, you can understand why. We learned more about the beauty of the West, and the boys continued to grow. Again I cannot guarantee everything is as good as it was in 2008, but the parks are there for you to (re)discover. Find the time, pick the places, do the research, and get out to the parks. Whether it is this itinerary or a variation, you will be ecstatic that you did. I know I was, and it once again stoked the desire to return to the West … eventually.

CHAPTER 3: EASTERN ODYSSEY #1
AN ACADIAN BREAK (2009)

PREPARATIONS

I knew we would not be going back out west until at least 2010, but I wanted to plan something for 2009 closer to home that did not require flying. I also wanted to take my parents somewhere special, so we gave them a trip for Christmas in 2008. Ever since my wife and I vacationed in Maine in 1992, I yearned to go back. This was our chance. All I had to do was find the right vacation time, get my parents to Pennsylvania, rent a large vehicle, and pick some memorable stops between home and Bar Harbor, Maine.

Step one was choosing when we would go. Because of soccer, hockey, theater, martial arts, fitness instruction, and other family activities, July was the logical choice again. I wanted to try to ensure good weather, and I also wanted to see cool fireworks on Independence Day. We would leave on Friday, July 3. We would return home late the following Thursday.

Step two was figuring out how we would get there from Pennsylvania. This was an easy one. We would rent a vehicle large enough for six people and their luggage and drive to Maine comfortably.

Step three was determining where we were going to visit and on what days. We needed to get to Bar Harbor by fireworks time on the Fourth of July. The first stop, New London, Connecticut, was just farther than halfway. It was near the water, a submarine base, and the

US Coast Guard Academy. From there we would drive to Bar Harbor for three days and three nights. I wanted to see some historical places on the way back, so we decided to stay in Rockport, Massachusetts, with possible stops at Plymouth Rock and Salem to see the witches. I wanted to cut the final drive down, and I originally chose Poughkeepsie, New York, for our last night out. I cannot remember why, but I later changed it to Mystic, Connecticut, just off I-95. So the trip route was set—New London, Connecticut, and a hopeful visit to the US Coast Guard Academy on Friday, July 3; Bar Harbor, Maine, and Acadia National Park on July 4 to 6; Rockport, Massachusetts, on July 7; Salem, Massachusetts, and Mystic, Connecticut, on July 8. *After all these years I was definitely looking forward to getting back to Bar Harbor and Acadia National Park!*

Step four was determining where we were going to stay. This trip was a departure from the previous national park trips, and I decided to take advantage of online travel/hotel sites that would give free nights after booking a certain number of rooms. This meant that we would be staying at some chain hotels. I also had to get two rooms at each stop to accommodate my parents, so the lodging cost would be doubled. The Holiday Inn in New London turned out to be a logical choice for the first night. It was right off I-95. After I talked to the people at the Days Inn near Bar Harbor, I settled on it. For the way home we found the Peg Leg Inn on the water in Rockport, Massachusetts. For our last night I finally settled on the Inn at Mystic to give my parents a room in a beautiful old house overlooking the water.

Step five was adding tours and additional activities on to the location visits. This was all Bar Harbor. I wanted to see a great Fourth of July fireworks show, and the Fish House Grill deck was the perfect spot. We also reserved two boat trips, the Bar Harbor Nature Cruise Tour and the longer Whale/Puffin Tour.

Step six was choosing certain meals to get a little fancy with. The only meal we reserved prior to the trip itself was the fireworks dinner at the Fish House Grill. This was to ensure we had prime seats for the fireworks. Other than that, we were looking forward to great seafood, and we had many places to choose from without having to make early reservations.

Step seven was choosing what vehicle we would drive around in. We reserved the largest SUV available so the six of us could ride comfortably.

Step eight was making sure we had the right supplies. We were not going to do a lot of hiking, but we would do some in the rugged areas of Acadia National Park, so the proper shoes were again important. We would need some warmer clothes for the boat rides, and we took sufficient electronics. Most of the trip was spent in populated areas, so we did not have to worry about the availability of snacks and drinks.

Step nine was budgeting for the Great Eastern Odyssey. The worksheet below is adapted from the spreadsheet file I use for all of our major trips. It shows the plans for the schedule, locations, activities, estimated costs and miles, actual costs, and the timing of the payments for each item. The need for two rooms each night added to the cost, but it was our Christmas present to my parents.

		2009 TRAVEL COSTS FOR OUR FUN				
DATES	DESTINATION	ITEM	ESTIMATES	ACTUAL PAID	DATES	MILES
07/09	Bar Harbor	Flights—Mom and Dad	469.18	469.18	03/15/2009	
07/09	Bar Harbor	Rental Car—Avis	503.00	503.00		
07/09	Bar Harbor	Hotel—New London Holiday Inn 07/03	348.12	348.12	04/14/2009	475
07/09	Bar Harbor	Hotel—Bar Harbor Days Inn (3 nights) 07/04-07/06	700.00	229.00		370
07/09	Bar Harbor	Hotel—Harborside Inn (07/05-07/06)		960.47		
07/09	Bar Harbor	Hotel—Rockport, MA (Peg Leg Inn) 07/07	373.00	373.00	04/11/2009	265
07/09	Bar Harbor	Hotel—Poughkeepsie	270.22	270.22	04/16/2009	
07/09	Bar Harbor	Misc	100.00			
07/09	Bar Harbor	Gas est. 2000 miles @ 20 mpg @ $2.50	250.00	250.00		
07/09	Bar Harbor	Dinners—6 nights	600.00	1,117.00		
07/09	Bar Harbor	Other Tours, Park Fees	150.00	50.00		
07/09	Bar Harbor	Nature Cruise Tour— Bar Harbor 07/05	151.00	151.00		
07/09	Bar Harbor	Whale/Puffin Tour— Bar Harbor 07/06	308.00	308.00		
07/09	Bar Harbor	Hotel—Mystic (The Inn at Mystic) 07/08	352.80	352.80	04/29/2009	145
07/09	Bar Harbor	Hotel—Poughkeepsie (Cancelled)	(270.22)	(270.22)	04/29/2009	
07/09	Bar Harbor			0.00		
07/09	Bar Harbor	Dinner—July 4th (Fish House Grill) 7:00 p.m.	390.00	150.00	05/17/2009	
07/09	Bar Harbor	Dinner—July 4th (Fish House Grill) 7:00 p.m.		300.00		
07/09	Bar Harbor	Cash	350.00	350.00		
07/09	Bar Harbor	Home				485
07/09	Bar Harbor					
July	3,868.47	Totals	$5,045.10	$5,911.57		1,740
Pre-	1,693.10					
Cash	350.00					
	5,911.57					

THE TRIP!

A number of things came up before and during the trip to make this an interesting story. Of course, just visiting Bar Harbor makes it interesting, but we had to deal with some issues. The year 2009 was an unusually wet year for the northeast. I monitored the weather constantly for many weeks before we were to leave, and the front seemed to just hover over Maine and the rest of the northeast. We would deal with it, but I was hoping for a break in the rain. The front would stay throughout our trip, but we would encounter some interesting timing of the weather conditions. Furthermore, my parents each had general health issues we needed to show concern for. As it turned out, we would have to deal with unforeseen health issues. The week before the trip, my father got sick with what turned out to essentially be walking pneumonia, and he was taking medicine for it. My mother also was suffering while she was walking, and we found out after the trip that she had broken bones in her foot. Regardless, they were determined to participate in our vacation, so they made the flight to Pittsburgh. The morning of the trip I was informed that the rental car company did not have the larger vehicle they promised me, and since I had not anticipated needing a roof rack, we were a little crammed in the SUV. Fortunately my packing skills made it so the driving situation was not too bad. While I knew we were heading to a beautiful destination, we had these issues to deal with before we ever got out of the driveway.

Day one was a drive day. Coming from a suburb southeast of Pittsburgh, our route started through the heart of Pennsylvania. This has charms that include the Laurel Highlands, some small mountains, rolling hills, trees, fields, etc., but it was not like some of our earlier drives out west. We made our way along Highways 22 and 99 up to I-80. We headed through New Jersey to I-95, and that took us through a little bit of New York and into Connecticut. The first day was a long 470 or so miles, but we broke up the monotony by reminiscing and listening to satellite radio and the "Forties on Four." My parents loved it, we survived it, and the kids turned on their MP3 players. The route along Long Island Sound in Connecticut was a nice drive with beautiful views of the water and some interesting industrial sights. We settled in to the Holiday Inn in New London, and we looked for a place to eat. Since we did not want to go out to a restaurant just yet, we ordered takeout from the steakhouse next to the hotel.

Saturday arrived, and we packed up for the drive to Maine. I like to schedule small sightseeing excursions to break up longer drives, but we really wanted to get to Bar Harbor. Thus, since it was around 370 miles that day, we decided to forego the stop at the Coast Guard Academy. We did, however, drive by the campus. That allowed us to see where it was and at least see some of the very pretty grounds of the academy. I had hoped to return someday. Interestingly enough, my niece would be attending it starting in the fall of 2014, so we probably will get back there. We bypassed Rhode Island for this part of the trip, and we went northeast on I-395, eventually cutting over to I-495. We took this until it reconnected with I-95 near the New Hampshire border. Central Connecticut and Massachusetts are very pretty places to drive, but the really cool stuff was coming soon. We spent about an hour in New Hampshire, another very pretty state, and then we entered Maine. Highways 1 and 9 run parallel to I-95 along the coast through many small towns. My wife and I actually took this route along the coast in 1992. If you are not bound by time, I highly recommend it.

As we headed northeast, we passed many small towns like Kittery, York, Ogunquit, Wells, and Kennebunkport. When we got to the Portland area, we branched off slightly to the east and got onto Highway 1. Falmouth, Freeport, Brunswick, and Bath were some of the really cool towns we went through along the water. Just past Bath is the town of Woolwich. There are rivers, waterways, marshes, and other water-related sights here, and we picked our first Maine eating establishment. It was lunchtime, and right off the highway we found the restaurant called the Taste of Maine. I am so glad we did. We all were looking forward to seafood, except my youngest son, who preferred steak. My father was still not feeling well, but we managed to get seated and enjoy a very tasty respite. If their food is still as good as it was in 2009, I definitely recommend it. We still had a couple of hours to go, but I want to note that Woolwich is near Boothbay Harbor. While we did not have the time to visit it on this trip, I highly recommend spending time there if you can. My wife and I stayed there for a few days during our

1992 trip, and it was really enchanting along the lines of Bar Harbor. I would love to tell you about that trip sometime.

The last leg of our journey to Bar Harbor continued along the water, with bays and harbors giving us more wonderful views. As Highway 1 became the Atlantic Highway, we passed Clam Cove, Rockport Harbor, and Penobscot Bay. At Bucksport, we turned east toward Ellsworth. Now we were getting close. Highway 1 continues east and northeast along the coast all the way to Canada, but we turned south onto Highway 3 toward Bar Harbor and Acadia National Park. The anticipation grew as we passed the airport, crossed the bridge, and turned east along Eastern Bay. Past Hulls Cove, Highway 3 became Eden Street, and we were right on the edge of the water. We passed one of the entrances to the Acadia National Park Loop Road. Just outside of Bar Harbor and near the Nova Scotia Ferry terminal were a number of hotels, condominiums, and motels, including the Days Inn. We got there and unloaded, anxious to relax and prepare for our first adventure watching fireworks on the water. We needed to get to the Fish House Grill around a quarter to seven for the dinner and fireworks show. The restaurant was on the pier at the corner where West Street meets Main Street in Bar Harbor, and the fireworks would be set off just beyond the main dock. West Street was a really nice place with houses, bed-and-breakfasts, resorts, and alleyways to the water. Main Street had shops and restaurants and led toward different access points to Acadia and the Park Loop Road.

The fireworks would go off at dark over the water, and we wanted to get a decent seat for dinner and the pyrotechnics. Unfortunately my father was still not ready to venture out, so he stayed back at the motel. Since we had to drive into town, I needed a place to park. A couple of blocks from the pier up West Street, there was the Harborside Hotel, Spa, and Marina. This was a very nice resort overlooking Frenchman's Bay, and it was a short walk to the pier and the shops on Main Street. Parking was in very short supply, but the Harborside offered their lot for twenty-five dollars. Rather than fight for a spot somewhere else, I decided to park there. It turned out to be a great decision for a number of reasons. The boys, my wife, my mother, and I parked and walked to the docks. We got situated at a picnic table with party favors, snacks, and drinks. I reserved and paid for dinners for six people, so I spoke with the staff about getting some food for my father. They were great, preparing a huge to-go box of seafood for him. I knew we had some time before the show, so I decided to take it to him. This is where Bar Harbor was going to get even better. I decided to stop in to the Harborside and check out room availability for our last two nights in town. I struck a deal for good rates, and they even waived the fireworks parking charge. I made the reservations, and this gave us upgraded lodging, easy parking, and much closer proximity to everything in town. I took the food to my father and told him about the plan. He was very happy and enjoyed the seafood.

I got back in time to celebrate the holiday with my family. The food was really good at the Fish House Grill, and the fireworks were actually pretty good. This was not a major show like some cities put on, but it was really enjoyable nonetheless. It had rained a little late in the afternoon and early in the evening, but my mother brought us good luck, and the rain held off throughout the fireworks show. As with every place I visit, I like to sample the local beers. This place offered another treat from a nearby brewery, the Shipyard Brewing Company out of Portland, Maine. My drink of choice was Shipyard Export Ale. It is described as "a full-bodied beer with a hint of sweetness up front, a subtle and distinctive hop taste, and a very clean finish." It was very tasty. I told everyone about my change in plans, and they were all excited. We hung around for a while after the fireworks ended, and then we made our way back to the motel. Sunday was going to bring more activities.

We checked out of the motel early and used our parking pass to park at the Harborside. Our first formal tour left the Ells Pier near the Fish House Grill that morning. We all were taking the Acadian Sightseeing and Nature Cruise to get a relaxing view of the beauty of the park by boat. This tour was only about two hours, and my father was up for the trip. We dressed accordingly with long pants and jackets, and once again my mother brought us good luck with the weather. There were a lot of clouds in the sky, but the sun shone through enough to make it a beautiful day. This cruise was on a tour boat with upper and lower decks. We rode along the coast in Frenchman's Bay, spying marinas, resorts, hotels, and many beautiful homes up past the rocky shoreline. We saw seals, porpoises, eagles, and other birds. We passed a beach with many people on it, and we passed islands with sea lions covering the rocks. We all were able to enjoy the animals, the sea breezes, and the beautiful nature throughout the park. We weaved through the Porcupine Islands in the bay, listening to the guide tell us about them. This was a very enjoyable introduction to a terrific place. After we got back, we walked the streets for a short time, and we had lunch at the West Street Café across from our hotel. This was a great place for lunch.

07/05/2009

Acadia National Park—Bar Harbor Coastline

We headed back to the Harborside and enjoyed some relaxing time there in our rooms, in the lobby, and at the pool. The sun had started to dominate the sky for now, so we took advantage of it. Later we decided to take advantage of the low tide and head out to Bar Island. Just up West Street was an alley where we could drive our vehicle out onto a sandbar and across to the island a few thousand yards away. We combined driving and walking to the island, stopping to relax and take pictures. We spent some time exploring the island, climbing and checking out bones and shells we had found. This was a lot of fun and not too demanding on my parents. Afterward, we took my parents back to rest at the hotel, and we decided to head up to Cadillac Mountain. This was Acadia National Park after all. The four of us weaved our way up the Park Loop Road and Cadillac Mountain Road, stopping at various observation points along the way. We arrived at the summit to marvel at the beauty of the surroundings. We did some hiking, took pictures, and read the signs that described the environment and history. We were going back there later on, but I wanted to get up there and let the boys run around a little. We headed back and met my parents. We walked up to the corner of West and Main, eating a wonderful dinner upstairs at the Quarterdeck Restaurant and enjoying the view. (Based on recent research, I believe the Quarterdeck is no longer there. Whatever restaurant is there now should give you a really nice view of the harbor.)

Early Monday morning was our whale-watching cruise. This was a much longer trip, so my father elected to stay at the Harborside. We dressed warm, walked down to the pier, and prepared to board. We bought some stomach medicine just in case we experienced seasickness. This boat tour was four hours, and it took us far out into the Gulf of Maine, closer to the open Atlantic. It was narrated, and we passed research points and other islands on our way. The main focus of this tour was to see whales and puffins. We also got to see seals, lighthouses, and other waterbirds. The puffins were colorful and really cool. They had unique shapes, and I was able to get some decent pictures. The sky was overcast, and it was windy with a lot of salty spray. Once the guide got us to the place where whales were thought to be, we navigated the area in search of whales. We were in luck, as numerous finback whales surfaced repeatedly, searching for food, air, and whatever else they search for. We saw single whales and groups of two and three. They did not get fully out of the water, but they continuously surfaced, sliding across the water effortlessly. This was another adventure we enjoyed, experiencing more of the ocean and what the Bar Harbor area offers. After several hours on the water, some close to seasickness, and a few periods of light rain, we headed back to Bar Harbor.

07/06/2009

Acadia National Park — Finback
Whale in Gulf of Maine

After we retrieved my father, we had lunch at the Fish House Grill and set out to explore Acadia National Park. We hit the loop road and made our way to the top of Cadillac Mountain. We wandered around, did some rock climbing, and took pictures of the surroundings. It is said that on most mornings this spot is where the sunrise can first be seen in the United States. The water, islands, mountains, and harbor were all available as spectacular views as the sun came out just enough to cast shadows and light up the peak. While we kept hiking to a minimum, I wanted to take my parents to Jordan Pond and the Jordan Pond House. This is a quaint and beautiful little lake along the western side of the Park Loop Road. It has a gift shop and a small restaurant where they serve tea and pastries in the afternoon. We got refreshments and sat on some of the benches in the large yard in front of the water. We walked along the trails and near the water, stopping to admire the scenery. After this, we made our way back to the Harborside and dropped off my parents.

We were preparing to have dinner at the hotel that night, but the four of us went on a little added excursion. We headed out of Bar Harbor and back onto the loop road, stopping at an overlook to snap the same picture I had taken seventeen years before. We made our way to Sand Beach, and all of the earlier beachgoers were gone. We had the beach to ourselves, and we roamed around, climbing the rocks that surrounded it, playing in the water, and pretending to be lifeguards. We then went to Thunder Hole, where the walkway to it had been upgraded since our 1992 visit. We made our way to the channel and watched as the water streamed in and caused thunderous noise as it crashed in and out. We climbed all over the rocks, checking out the different terrain and the water. Eventually we made our way back to the hotel and had a fabulous dinner there with my parents.

07/06/2009

Acadia National Park — Park Loop Road Picture

We really enjoyed Bar Harbor and Acadia National Park, though there is so much more to see. The Park Loop Road takes you around the eastern third of Mount Desert Island. *You should definitely study maps of the park and research the features.* If you venture west on Highways 3, 102,

198, and 233, you will get to even more beautiful locations and natural wonders on the island. There are many ponds, coves, towns, mountains, and rocks to discover. In 1992, my wife and I did this, finding the Bass Harbor Head Lighthouse and Somes Sound, the only fjord on the East Coast of the United States, among other places. We even got over to Seal Cove by accident after our exhaust pipe fell off on top of Cadillac Mountain. The best mechanic on the island was there, and he fixed up our very loud Jetta. We saw the sunrise on Cadillac Mountain and walked the streets of Bar Harbor, truly enjoying our stay at the Manor House Inn Bed and Breakfast. While you realize that there is plenty to do and see, just getting to Acadia National Park and Bar Harbor will make you happy that you did.

On Tuesday morning of July 7, it was time for us to leave the harbor. We had about five hours to get to Rockport, Massachusetts, and we were not in any particular hurry. Interestingly, as soon as we got on the highway, the rain started again. The drive west through Maine would be a wet one, and we were not sure how the weather in Rockport would be. After we came back on Highway 1, we jumped onto I-295 near Brunswick, and shortly after that we made our first pit stop of the day in Freeport, Maine. My wife and I had stopped here in 1992, and it was home to many outlet stores housed in a picturesque little town. Freeport is also the home of the headquarters of L.L.Bean. If you are an L.L.Bean enthusiast, you have to stop at this store. We spent some time there, going through the many departments and taking pictures with the giant boot outside the front doors.

We got back on I-295, moved over to I-95, headed out of Maine, and drove through New Hampshire and into Massachusetts. Our destination was the tip of the distinctive peninsula thirty-five miles northeast of Boston. We eventually jumped on Highway 128 and made our way east past Manchester and Gloucester (pronounced Glawstuh) out to Rockport. One of the cool things out here is that everything is *wicked*. On the corner of Beach and King Streets in Rockport, across the street from Front Beach and Sandy Bay, there is the Peg Leg Inn. This really cool bed-and-breakfast has numerous rooms on multiple levels, and the porch view is beautiful. Amazingly, as soon as we got there, the rain stopped, and the skies partially cleared. We were able to head across the street and down onto the beach, walking on the sand and into the ocean water. We were not prepared to do any actual swimming, but just being there was awesome. We spent quality time on the shore and built up an appetite for dinner. We were a short distance from the village of Rockport, and we parked on one of the winding streets. We hit some shops, and then we found the Fish Shack restaurant. It had a pretty view of the water, and the food was excellent. My father was very happy with the scallops, and I enjoyed some fabulous beer from Boston's Harpoon Brewery, Harpoon IPA. We saw some rain through the large restaurant windows during our meal, and we headed back to the Peg Leg Inn shortly after that.

07/07/2009

Rockport, Massachusetts — Beach

We had one more day of vacation left, not including the drive home on Thursday. I wanted to cut the final drive down, and I had originally booked a hotel in Poughkeepsie, New York. I changed that after I found the enchanting location of Mystic, Connecticut. Of course, this did not cut the final drive down, but it made for a relatively easy drive from Rockport. We left the Peg Leg and drove along the water a short time, making a late morning tourist stop in Salem, Massachusetts. The history here is of the witch trials in the 1690s and the related early colonial events. We walked through an area where historical buildings still stand, and we took a tour of the Salem Witch Museum. We learned some interesting things there, including what *stoning* was and that one of the *afflicted* in 1692 had a last name of Phelps. Related? Maybe. We had lunch, jumped on I-95, bypassed Boston, and took in the scenery as we drove through the state of Rhode Island. A short distance into Connecticut was the town of Mystic. It is located where the Mystic River meets the Block Island Sound just before the Atlantic Ocean. Our lodging would be the Inn at Mystic. This was a really nice multibuilding estate overlooking Mystic Harbor. Our room was in the lower section with a motel-like entrance. My parents' room was in the historic Haley Mansion on the hill just above us. This was a really cool structure, and their room was in the front with a great view of the harbor. They could even walk out onto the roof and relax in deck chairs, enjoying the beautiful afternoon weather. The boys played on the piano downstairs, and we strolled on the huge porch surrounding the mansion. The rain had cleared out to the east, so our stay in Mystic was picture-perfect. It was so nice that you could have made a movie there.

07/08/2009

Mystic, Connecticut

Our final day was a long driving day. We had nearly five hundred miles to travel. We took a nice drive through the town of Mystic, and then we got on I-95. This took us back the way we had originally come through Connecticut, New York, New Jersey, and Pennsylvania. We listened to the Forties on Four, talked about the trip, and rejoiced in the fact that my father was feeling better.

Family at Acadia National Park

SUMMATION

So the Eastern Odyssey was in the books. *We enjoyed a week of Atlantic Coast travel to New London, Connecticut; Bar Harbor, Maine; Acadia National Park; Rockport, Massachusetts; and Mystic, Connecticut!* This was a somewhat different trip from those out west, but it still entailed choosing a fabulous central destination and hitting some highlights along the way. We had to deal with health issues and the weather, and we encountered actual silver linings throughout the trip. It is important to note that there are many awe-inspiring places along the northeastern Atlantic coastline, and Bar Harbor is at the top of the list for me. If you like nature, I highly recommend doing the research and looking at this place to spend as much time as you have available. While it was not out west, it was still worthy of many superlatives. We got to spend time with my parents in a fantastic place, and it was a great way to fill in the summer between western odysseys.

CHAPTER 4: WESTERN ODYSSEY #3
TOP OF THE COUNTRY (2010)

PREPARATIONS

Planning for this adventure started in 2009 not long after we returned from Maine. However, the seeds for it were planted well before that. When my wife and I flew to Seattle in 1994, we experienced some spectacular scenery and sights. On that trip we did not get across the water to the west to Olympic National Park. In the 2007–2008 time frame, some friends also described for me their journeys to the beautiful Glacier National Park in Montana. Since these two northern treasures were only about 650 miles apart, they were natural bookends for another fantastic Western Odyssey. This was going to be an awesome trip and maybe even the best trip ever!

Step one was choosing when we would go. Just like you, we have had to juggle priorities and schedules more and more as the kids have grown up. Because of charity, soccer, hockey, football, coaching, travels, theater, martial arts, fitness instruction, and other activities, July was the choice once again. Weather is also a factor when you are dealing with snowfall and the mountains. The main park road in Glacier is often closed into July, so this helped with our timing choice. We chose July 17 as our start date.

Step two was figuring out how we would get there from Pennsylvania. Again by January I had amassed enough miles on my credit card to fly us west for free. The flights to Seattle would be Saturday evening, getting us to Seattle in time to stay the night before heading to Olympic. For multiple reasons the airport in Missoula, Montana, would be our return flight location. This would reduce our flight choices, but we would still be able to squeeze out seven full days of vacation.

Step three was determining where we were going to visit and on what days. Olympic is an amazing place where you have multiple ecosystems within a short distance of one another. There are rain forests, lakes, ocean beaches with tidal pools, snowcapped mountains, old growth forests, rivers, and vampire towns all contained on the peninsula. The main park roads are paved, so we basically had to map out where we wanted to go and just go there. I also wanted to get back to one other place not in the park. We visited the Mount St. Helens volcano in 1994 (fourteen years after the eruption), and I wanted to see what it was like another sixteen years later. That would be a partial day trip out of the park. On the way to Glacier, we would stop at a few places, depending on the time. While in Glacier, I wanted to get to Logan Pass at the top of the "Going to the Sun Road." I also wanted to get into Canada and see as many mountainous areas as possible. There are many incredible sights in Glacier, and I was determined to see as much as we could in a couple of days. So the trip route was set—Olympic National Park, Mount St. Helens National Volcanic Monument, I-90 across three states, and Glacier National Park in the United States and Canada. This was shaping up to be a fantastic adventure.

Step four was determining where we were going to stay. The first night was a quick stay because we arrived in Seattle late at night. We chose the Red Roof Inn right near the airport. There are many places to stay in Olympic National Park, and each has proximity to great spots. While I was looking for lodging in the park, I came across these possibilities: Kalaloch Lodge, Lake Quinault Lodge, Lake Crescent Lodge, Sol Duc Hot Springs Resort, and numerous places in Port Angeles. I decided I wanted to stay right on the ocean, so I chose Kalaloch Lodge. The travel day between parks brought me to the Red Lion Hotel in Kalispell, Montana, and the final night would be at the Days Inn in Missoula, Montana. The two nights in Glacier gave me numerous choices, and I ended up picking the Prince of Wales Hotel near Waterton, Canada, and the Glacier Park Lodge in the southeastern part of the park. All of these were excellent choices for multiple reasons.

Step five was adding tours and additional activities on to the location visits. With all of the places to visit in Olympic, I chose to reserve a guided tour that would take us rafting on the Elwha River. In Glacier, I also chose a guided tour flying a helicopter over the mountains. These were going to be fun and memorable.

Step six was choosing certain meals to get a little fancy with. I actually did not reserve any dinners, figuring that we would not have any problems with lodge restaurants and the surrounding locations.

Step seven was choosing what vehicle we would drive around in. Since we would be driving on paved roads virtually everywhere, I opted for a sedan to improve gas mileage and reduce overall cost. Again, with the rental starting and ending in different locations, it would still be more expensive than if it was being dropped off back at the same place.

Step eight was making sure we had the right supplies. This was pretty standard, though we would be experiencing cooler weather in both locations. We made sure we took long pants, sweatshirts, and jackets to go along with shorts and T-shirts. Our Merrell shoes were still going strong, and the boys brought what fit them at the time. I did upgrade the digital camera situation, adding a Digital SLR camera with an additional zoom lens. Thus, even though my picture-taking skills were not the greatest, I was hoping the camera would compensate for it and produce some memorable photos.

Step nine was budgeting for the great trip to the northwest. The following worksheet is adapted from the spreadsheet file I use for all of our major trips. It shows the plans for the schedule, locations, activities, estimated costs and miles, actual costs, and the timing of the payments for each item. This vacation would be a little more expensive, but it would be worth it. These two destinations are truly special.

2010 TRAVEL COSTS FOR OUR FUN						
DATES	DESTINATION	ITEM	ESTIMATES	PAID-VISA	DATES	MILES
07/10	West Swing III	Flights — add'l costs	30.00	30.00	1/21/10	
07/10	West Swing III	Hotel — First Night (Red Roof Inn)	78.08	78.08	2/25/10	
07/10	West Swing III	Kalaloch Lodge — Olympic National Park (3)	382.85	382.85	1/21/10	175
07/10	West Swing III	Kalaloch Lodge — Olympic National Park (3)	759.70	759.70	7/21/10	680
07/10	West Swing III	Lodging—Kalispell (1)	149.00	149.00	3/01/10	680
07/10	West Swing III	Lodging — Glacier — Prince of Wales (1)	496.48	496.48	2/25/10	125
07/10	West Swing III	Lodging — Glacier — Glacier Park Lodge (1)	251.64	251.64	2/25/10	100
07/10	West Swing III	Hotel — last Night (Days Inn Missoula) (1)	102.00	102.00	7/24/10	200
07/10	West Swing III	Flights — Bags	25.00	25.00	7/17/10	
07/10	West Swing III	Flights — Bags	25.00	25.00	7/25/10	
07/10	West Swing III	Rental Car	1,039.71	1,039.71	7/25/10	
07/10	West Swing III	Rafting trip	250.00	258.82	7/20/10	
07/10	West Swing III	Helicopter Tour — Glacier 07/22/10	880.00	898.95	7/22/10	
07/10	West Swing III	Spa — Massages (GPL)	156.00	156.00	7/24/10	
07/10	West Swing III	Passports	230.00	230.00	5/28/10	
07/10	West Swing III	Miles Estimate — 2,200				
07/10	West Swing III	Park Fees — Olympic (Cash)	15.00			
07/10	West Swing III	Park Fees — Glacier (Cash)	25.00			
07/10	West Swing III	Meals estimate 07/18-07/24 (est. $120/day)	840.00	844.97	7/10	
07/10	West Swing III	Misc. Food	250.00	0.00		
07/10	West Swing III	Misc., Nick Knacks, Shirts	150.00	233.95	7/10	
07/10	West Swing III	Gas (estimate 28 mpg x $3 x 2,200 miles)	235.71	330.28	7/10	
07/10	West Swing III					
07/10	West Swing III	Cash—Initial	350.00		7/17/10	

2010 TRAVEL COSTS FOR OUR FUN						
DATES	DESTINATION	ITEM	ESTIMATES	PAID-VISA	DATES	MILES
07/10	West Swing III	Cash — ATMs on trip	102.00			
07/10	West Swing III	Parking — Airport 07/25/10 (8 days)	64.00	**64.00**	7/25/10	
Aug Visa	4,738.38	Totals	$6,887.17	**$6,356.43**		1,960
Pre-Visa	1,618.05					
Cash	492.00					
Actual Totals	6,848.43					

THE TRIP!

Planning for this trip was a lot of fun. While there were only two main destinations, each had many great features and spots to experience. The flights and lodging were secured nearly six months before the actual vacation, so a good portion of the work was done early. Since we were heading to the Olympic Peninsula, where the *Twilight* movies were set, we rented and watched the original *Twilight* movie the night before we flew out. We had not yet seen it, so we wanted to get a feel for the area around Forks, Washington. It was entertaining. Anticipation grew steadily, and we flew out on the evening of July 17. Even with the three-hour time-zone change, we got to SeaTac pretty late. We were able to get our car and head over to the hotel to rest for the drive on Sunday.

After we checked out that morning, we had about 175 miles to drive to get to Kalaloch Lodge. Much of this was on slower highways through smaller towns. *You want to become very familiar with the Olympic park map.* It shows the features and areas you can experience as you venture through the park. It is also helpful to take an atlas, weather forecasts, topographical hiking maps, and tide pool charts for the ocean beaches. It is also helpful to obtain a copy of the latest Park newspaper *The Bugler*. Use these tools as you read this, and it will give you a clear picture of where you can go. We headed down I-5 to Highway 101, the main Olympic Park road. After short jogs on Highways 8 and 12, we were back on 101. We passed some nice little towns on the waterways, and then we entered national forest, Indian reservation, and Pacific coastline areas. There are many trailheads and side routes on 101, and there are lumber companies with massive piles of logs. We passed Lake Quinault and the town of Queets and hit the coast on our way to the Kalaloch Lodge. We got there and checked it out briefly before we headed across the street to the ranger station. This is where we obtained useful information about the park, and they confirmed our tide schedule readings. We had just enough time to get to Rialto Beach and explore the tidal pools before high tide.

We would have to drive about sixty-five miles to get to the beach, so we set out. Apparently I was in too much of a hurry, as a friendly police officer pulled me over almost immediately. Fortunately I somehow managed to not get a ticket, and we were on our way again but at a slower pace. My advice is to make sure you try to obey the park speed limits. Not far from Kalaloch near Ruby Beach, we turned inland to drive around some of the vast wilderness area. We passed the Hoh Rain Forest access road, multiple rivers, and many trees. Shortly after we drove through Forks, a place where we would stop again, we turned toward the ocean on Highway 110, LaPush Road. About two-thirds of the way to the ocean, we veered right on Mora Road, which took us to the trailhead at Rialto Beach.

We got out for our first hike in Olympic along the Pacific Ocean coastline. It was not cold, but we were socked in with no sun and continued wind gusts off the ocean. We made our way to the shoreline with the goal of hiking to and exploring the "Hole-In-The-Wall" a couple of miles up the beach. This was an example of a sea stack. Sea stacks are giant rocks sitting on or near the shore, depending on the tide. Because of the hole, it could also be technically called an arch. As we hiked, we encountered huge driftwood trees strewn all over the beach. Many were ashen white, while others were newer with some hint of color left. They offered opportunities to climb and take cool pictures. There were also many white and gray trees still standing farther from the water, constantly buffeted by the ocean and stripped of much of their color. Not far beyond these were living trees of the forest in varying degrees of color. The sand, stones, driftwood, trees, and ground cover gave us a beautiful earthen color contrast as we looked inland from the beach. There were rock islands and sea stacks out in the water, and the wind-swept waves crashed near us continuously as we walked. There were stones, shells, fish and bird remains, and other beach-related things, and we eventually came to some sea stacks that were accessible to us. We climbed and explored, sometimes wandering into the water.

Olympic National Park — Rialto
Beach Driftwood Tree

We eventually made it to the Hole-in-the-Wall and ventured onto its surfaces. It was an extension off the sandy beach, and we were able to walk freely through the hole during low tide. In the many tide pools we saw sea anemone, various plants, and many colorful sea stars or starfish. The starfish were often in clumped groups, and they came in bright colors, including orange, purple, and reddish brown. There were many piles of mussels and barnacles on the rocks, adding to the different colors dotting the gray rocks. Even though the sun never peaked out, the sights were amazing. Of course, if you can get here when the sun is out, you will enjoy it in another light. We could have gone much farther up the coast, but the tide would have eventually forced us back. Besides, we still needed to check in, and we were getting hungry. We made our way back to our car, stopping occasionally to explore the wonders of the waterline. One really cool thing to me was the presence of plant life and fully grown trees on top of some of the sea stacks. With the wind, salt, and storms, you would think they would not have a chance to thrive, but there they were. This was an amazing introduction to the first of numerous ecosystems in Olympic National Park.

Olympic National Park — Rialto Beach Sea Stacks

We headed back to Highway 101 and turned south, making our way into Forks. Here it was clear and sunny. Again this was in the middle of the popularity of the *Twilight* movies, and we decided to stop at a store on the main street called "Dazzled by Twilight." This novelty shop had everything *Twilight* you could think of, and we wandered around and marveled at the Bella, Edward, and Jacob merchandise. We took pictures of my wife and son with a life-size cardboard Edward, and then we took off for Kalaloch Lodge. (Recent research has told me that the "Dazzled" store is no longer open in Forks.) We eventually checked into the lodge, unloading into our cottage on the bluff that overlooked the ocean. After a tasty dinner at the restaurant in the lodge, we visited the convenient general store on the premises, and then we retired to the cottage. We rested for the events of the next day, and I enjoyed drinking a Redhook ESB from the Redhook Brewing Company, one of my favorite beers of all time.

The plan for Monday morning was to head out of the park to see the Mount St. Helens National Volcanic Monument. It was approximately two hundred miles from Kalaloch, so we departed after breakfast. As we headed inland off the Olympic Peninsula, we made a stop at Lake Quinault for a quick hike to see a tree. Lake Quinault is a natural lake formed by a glacier long ago. It is surrounded by the Quinault Indian Reservation, the Colonel Bob Wilderness, and the Olympic National

Forest. The temperate rain forest around the lake receives an average of twelve feet of rain each year. Just before the lake is North Shore Road, and a short distance off 101 is a turnout and the trailhead for the Quinault Big Cedar. I had read this was a big tree, so I wanted us to witness its enormity. The trail is not long, and there are steps and bridges in some places to aid with the elevation change. During the walk we saw many trees with moss draped all over them. This is a hallmark of the rain forests in Olympic, and it looks really cool. Green ferns and ground cover along with colorful berries added contrast to the brown tree wood. We made our way through large and tall trees, both standing and fallen. We got to the Big Cedar tree, and it was humongous. It is more than 170 feet high and more than sixty feet around with moss and new trees actually growing out of it. It is hollowed out, so you can walk inside the trunk and look up to the sky. We checked it out for a while, taking some scale pictures, and then we made our way back down the trail to our car.

Olympic National Park — Quinault Big Cedar Tree

We drove on 101 toward I-5, heading south when we got to it. After a few hours of driving, we exited southeast on Highway 505, eventually turning east on Highway 504, which is also called Spirit Lake Highway. This took us to the Johnston Ridge Observatory, where we could see the front of the Mount St. Helens National Volcanic Monument. The 1980 eruption had blown a few thousand feet off the top of the mountain, forever changing the landscape as far as the eye can see. My wife and I had been here sixteen years before, and it had definitely changed since then. The surrounding valleys had much more greenery, and many of the fallen trees had decomposed into the soil, further feeding it for new growth. However, the immediate area between us and the mountain still looked like moonscape. There was still snow on the peaks, and the slowly growing lava dome was ever-present inside the mouth of the volcano. There were also spots where blown-over trees still covered the hillsides, looking like toothpicks strewn all over the ground. We wandered around the observatory area, taking pictures and checking out the exhibits inside. The bright sky was a fantastic backdrop to the crater. Since this eruption was so recent and so devastating, it was even more interesting to see this awesome spectacle of nature. Knowing the history of the mountain, I highly recommend seeing this place in person, if you are able to make the time.

Mount St. Helens National Volcanic Monument

We headed back the way we came, and as we approached Lake Quinault, we turned onto South Shore Road. Up this road you will find numerous rain forest trails, campgrounds, Lake Quinault Lodge, the Rain Forest Resort, and the World's Largest Sitka Spruce. We stopped at the parking lot for the first trail. It was called the Rain Forest Nature Trail. This relatively short trail is described as "the rain forest in a nutshell," and we ventured onto the well-maintained trail. We encountered tall trees, ferns, streams, moss-covered branches, waterfalls, and the occasional small animal. The sun was below the treetops but still visible through the forest, casting eerie shadows and light beams throughout our hike. I am sure morning and midday also offer their own version of beauty in this serene place, so multiple trips to the rain forests would be rewarding. One thing that is really cool is the array of different fallen trees and their many shapes. We explored stumps, trunks, hollows, and full-sized trees scattered about on the forest floor. My wife and son also found a large banana slug making its way across a downed tree. These are slow, large, and noticeable creatures, and they glisten in the light. The additional trails and huge trees along the South Shore Road should be featured destinations in any future trip to Olympic, and you should try to hike them at different times of the day for varied lighting. We made our way back to the car and headed back to Kalaloch as the sun disappeared.

Olympic National Park—Quinault Rain Forest

Tuesday was going to be a busy day, with the reserved raft trip being one of the highlights. We headed out early, going clockwise and north on Highway 101. It was approximately ninety miles to Port Angeles, where the park entrance and the road to Hurricane Ridge were located. Our rafting trip was scheduled for late afternoon on the Elwha River, which was just before Port Angeles. Before we headed inland from the coast, we made a quick stop a short way up the road at Ruby Beach. We did not go too far, but we got a quick peak at more of the coastline and more awesomeness. Not far from Port Angeles, we made a pit stop at a shop next to Lake Crescent, another beautiful glacier-formed lake. We took some pictures and then enjoyed the winding ride along the lake as we made our way up 101. Port Angeles is a nice city, and we made our way through it to the park entrance. We then drove the seventeen-mile winding mountain road to Hurricane Ridge. Most of the drop-offs were hidden by tall trees growing along the road, so the mountain driving did not bother me too much. We stopped a few times to take some pictures of the nature surrounding us, and we enjoyed the multiple tunnels we passed through on the way. At the visitor's center, we roamed around the gift shop, got some food at the grill, and ventured out onto the grounds outside the building to take in the stunning scenery. We saw deer along the road and in the parking lot, roaming among the people and cars. We took pictures and video of the snowcapped mountains, the alpine forests, the wildflowers, the meadows, and the valleys. We marveled at Mount Olympus in the distance, which was almost eight thousand feet high and surrounded by peaks and glaciers.

Olympic National Park—Hurricane Ridge

After a while we left the mile-high elevation to hike up higher. We drove a short distance farther and hit the Hurricane Hill trailhead. We set out along the mountainside and through the trees and meadows, stopping occasionally to take in the beauty. Snow often covers this area well into June, and we came across some remaining pockets of thick snow as we hiked around. We got to the top of the hill without my younger son. He decided to lay down next to the trail shortly before we got to the summit. People would stop and ask him if he was okay, and he would just wave them on with a smile. My older son spent time watching a deer feed near snow drifts. My wife straddled the edges of the cliffs. I took more pictures and gazed in the distance at Port Angeles, the Strait of Juan de Fuca, and Victoria, Canada. After the exhilarating trek we hiked back to the car. I could have spent a lot of time here; however, we were on a timetable, and the rafting trip was coming up soon.

The Olympic Raft and Kayak Company offers river rafting and kayak tours in Olympic. I had reserved an Elwha River raft trip months before, and we backtracked from Port Angeles a short distance to the Elwha access road and the headquarters. The midafternoon trips lasted several hours over five to six miles of the river. The dam removal project was occurring as we visited, but the water past it was not yet accessible to rafters. The river is fed by glacial runoff, so it is very cold at around 50 degrees. Even though the rapids are mainly class twos with some mild class threes, we were convinced to rent wet suits, waterproof booties, and gloves for the ride. There were multiple rafting groups, and we were transported to the starting point by van. Fortunately our raft only had the four of us and our guide. She was a petite female college student from the East working here for the summer. The boys liked her a lot. The large rubber raft was fun to paddle in, and we navigated through mild rapids and gorgeous back country. Near the halfway point the group made landfall for a brief rest. Rafters were encouraged to make the plunge into the cold water, knowing the wet suits would keep them mostly dry. Three of us took the ice-water challenge while I took pictures. Everyone echoed how refreshing it was. I took pictures.

Shortly after we resumed our voyage, we turned into an area where there were some large rock obstructions and an increased current. The other rafts got past the rocks. For us it happened fast. My younger son lost his paddle, and we somehow quickly strayed into the rocks. Our raft wedged right in between two large boulders, and we started taking on water as the raft was lodged at a sixty degree angle. We tried some bouncing techniques, but we were stuck. Our guide was not wearing a wet suit, and she thought maybe she could push eight hundred pounds of people and a raft off the rocks. She slipped off the slick rock into the water, and I sprang into rescue mode. I jumped on the rocks and grabbed her hand, lifting her up out of the water and into the raft. We then applied physics, geometry, and other scientific principles to shift everyone while we slowly moved the raft off the rocks. We finally broke free and floated toward the other rafters, who were all watching in a kind of stunned silence and wondering what had just happened. Fortunately they had retrieved our paddle, and we all got back on course with something more to talk about. We found out that the gear was not totally waterproof, but we did not have far to go. We beached the rafts, loaded them onto the vans, and headed back to the headquarters. We thanked our guide, changed our clothes, and hit the road with another story for future memory.

It was now getting late in the afternoon, and we had a long drive back toward Kalaloch. We stopped briefly in Forks for gas, and we grabbed dinner at Sully's Drive-In. The burgers were a welcome treat, and we sat next to the table that had a sign saying, "Reserved for Edward and Bella." About thirteen miles down 101 is the access road to the Hoh Rain Forest. Unfortunately the Hoh hike would end up being lost as darkness descended upon us. Nevertheless, I made a decision to take the eighteen-mile road so that I could say, "I was there." This turned out to be a great call. It was a beautiful night, and the moon was bright in the sky. We could not travel at a very high speed here, so we were able to take in the surroundings as we drove. There were many trees, bushes, and tall hedgerows really close to the road, and the shadows and fog made for an eerie atmosphere. At times it felt like we were in a tunnel as we wound around ghostly curves under canopies of branches. We could see into valleys and into the Hoh River, and some spots caused us to do double takes to try to figure out what we actually saw. The boys were asleep in the backseat, so my wife and I enjoyed the ethereal experience together.

We eventually made our way to the visitor center and campground, and I parked near the trailhead. I left the car running and ran up the trail to the first sign to take a picture of it. As I set up for the picture, mosquitoes chowed on me as they always like to do. I quickly took the picture and ran back to the car. We made our way back toward 101, enjoying the moonlit route on the return trip. We got back to Kalaloch and settled in at the cabin, preparing for the long drive the next day. Again Hoh is one of the big attractions in Olympic, and I wish I had more time to get there. You need to plan accordingly so you can experience it adequately during the daylight, but a nighttime drive along Upper Hoh Road will rouse your senses. I can really only say, "I was there," but as an cyborg famously said in a 1984 movie, "I'll be back!"

Olympic National Park—Hoh Rain Forest Sign

Wednesday was the big drive day. We had nearly seven hundred miles to cover, so we had to load, check out, and get on the road early. We did, however, make a little time for some pit stops. Prior to leaving, my younger son and I took a quick drive up the road to Ruby Beach. We took the trail through the woods to the beach and checked out the drift log piles and climbable sea stacks. We were not there long, but it was a great little farewell to the ocean. Ruby is one of many beaches with access points along Highway

101 that provide opportunities to have fun on the ocean's edge. We got back, checked out of Kalaloch Lodge, and headed inland. We made another diversion onto South Shore Road, stopping to take a short walk around the grounds of the Lake Quinault Lodge and the lake itself. This is a really cool old building with a large front yard that leads to the lake. When I return, I will check into staying here. We left and made our way to I-5 North, veering northeast toward I-90 near Tacoma. To our right Mount Rainier towered prominently in the sun, giving us another awesome sight to see as we made our way east. Not long after we merged onto I-90 we came to the town of Snoqualmie. My wife and I had visited there in 1994, and we hiked at the bottom of the waterfall. I wanted to see it again, so we stopped for a break. We found that a lot of work had been done to the falls area with walkways, overlooks, shops, and other amenities to make the visit a fun one. We took some pictures of the waterfall, reminisced, got a snack, and moved on again.

While we had a long way to go, the scenery through central Washington made it a much more enjoyable ride. We went through mountains and national forests, around lakes and rivers, over bridges, and through small towns. The natural contrasts here are definitely worth seeing. At lunchtime we stopped for burritos and gas, and later we saw a massive wind turbine farm in eastern Washington not far from Spokane. Passing into Idaho for the short drive across its northern peninsula was another source of natural beauty. The Coeur d'Alene area offers lakes, national forests, mountains, and a fast speed limit. It looked like a fantastic place to visit some day. Entering Montana continued the gorgeous scenery. After a while we exited I-90 onto Route 135 East and then Route 200 to the northwest. These roads ran along rivers and through forests, hills, and mountains, continuously giving us things to look at. We finally turned onto Route 28 Northeast, making our way toward Kalispell. It was getting dark, and we stopped at a casino for supplies, taking some sunset pictures along the way. As it got dark, we encountered some road construction, even having to wait for leader cars to take us through one section. I assume the construction is finished by now … hopefully. Route 28 ended at Highway 93, which is next to Flathead Lake. This was a really nice-looking area just south of Kalispell, and it could be part of another future vacation stop. We finally arrived at our final destination of the night, the Red Lion Hotel in Kalispell. This was a conveniently located place with nice rooms and amenities. We relaxed, grabbed some food, and rested up for the next adventure. We were anxious to go to Glacier.

Thursday was our wedding anniversary, and I had some awesome presents planned for my wife. We had breakfast at the hotel and then headed up Highway 2 toward our first adventure of the day. I had booked a morning helicopter tour with Kruger Helicop-Tours. They are located just before Glacier National Park's southwest entrance, and they offer half-hour and full-hour flights for up to four passengers. I opted for the full hour, anticipating the additional glaciers and sights included with it. I rode up front with the pilot, and my wife and boys were in the backseat. We all had our headsets on, and we took off into the park. This was a fantastic vantage point to see the park from, as we flew over valleys, lakes, forests, meadows, rivers, streams, waterfalls, and mountains that only hard-core hikers would ever see from the ground. We hovered right next to glacial snow and ice packs, and as we came up over peaks, the sudden wind changes would cause a distinctly different whooping sound from the helicopter rotors. Sculpted gray mountains morphed from snow cover to rock to lush green valleys below with beautiful glacial lakes sparkling in the sunlight. We briefly crossed into Canada and the Waterton section of the park, and we flew over the main park road. Unfortunately the weather did not fully cooperate, and we hit patches of rain in the northern section of the park. This limited our penetration into Canada, but the sensation of flying in a bubble with the rain pelting us was pretty interesting. The pilot named numerous glaciers, lakes, and features of the vast expanse. He also pointed out places where he was involved with rescues, bear relocations, body discoveries, and other park-related calamities. It gave me multiple examples of where not to hike. The continental divide was a topic for discussion, as the park is a central point where the Columbia, Saskatchewan, and Missouri rivers carry water off in different directions. The climax of the trip was the hovering visit to Beaver Chief Falls. It is listed in the World Waterfall Database as nearly thirteen hundred feet high with three drops and multiple lakes involved. This area is accessible on foot, but it is a long, strenuous hike. Seeing it from above was really awesome. Even under an overcast sky, the magnificence of the location was abundantly evident. Passing so close to the sides of the mountains makes it easier to see the patterns etched into them from glaciers, wind, water, and the continuous freezing and thawing. We eventually made our way back to our launch pad and thanked the pilot. Although apparent user error screwed up my camera during the flight, I managed to get a lot of great pictures over a fantastic location. Who touched my camera?

Glacier National Park—Beaver
Chief Falls from Helicopter

Next to the helicopter tour place was a western store with all kinds of Native American gifts and western apparel. We had some fun and met some interesting people there, and then we started off toward the west entrance of Glacier National Park. I had read about the Going to the Sun Road and was slightly wary of the narrow mountain driving, but I was determined to enjoy it. The first eight miles or so are in low country along Lake McDonald, which is a gorgeous body of water. We briefly drove around the Lake McDonald Lodge to check it out. We stopped at a few turnouts and found one that gave us a nice little hiking opportunity. The trailhead led to a bridge, and we could walk across it and under it to explore rocks and the water just downstream from a snowmelt waterfall. It was really nice, and I would like to see it in springtime when the runoff is much greater. We continued on the park road, and made our way up into the mountains. We passed through tunnels and took mobile pictures of the peaks and natural features as we went. It had been cloudy but turned to light rain, robbing some of the color of our surroundings. We made it past "the Loop" and stopped at the "Weeping Wall" and some snowpacks to enjoy the scenery and take pictures. There were pockets of construction on the road, and the workers would sometimes seem to defy gravity, working across the low retaining walls. Water cascading down runoff ravines on the sides of mountains was a common sight, and there was even a really cool place where a bridge was built right over the water flow. As we continued our elevation climb, we encountered more snowpacks near the road, and when we got to the Logan Pass Visitor Center, the rain had subsided. It was still overcast, and we set out on some of the trails. There are many extensive trails emanating from here, but we stuck to the shorter hikes. At more than 6,600 feet, we were really high up, but we were surrounded by peaks towering thousands more feet above us. We walked through snow, trees, and wildflowers, enjoying the beauty and the sun trying to peak through.

As we set out on the final third of the park road, the clouds broke, and the sun shone on more flowers, alpine trees and valleys, snowy mountains, and water streams. We made stops to experience rushing water, colorful stones, trees, plants, and snow-spotted mountains all around us. It turned into a beautiful day as we made our way along Saint Mary Lake. We stopped there to enjoy the aqua water and the mountains on the other side. We could see the contrast of forest sections that had been burned right next to trees untouched by fire, and small animals crossed our path. We stopped at the Rising Sun Motor Inn for a break, and we enjoyed one of the delicacies of the area—huckleberries. After we exited the park through the east entrance, we stopped at a place recommended by a colleague who had visited Glacier not long before us, the Park Café. This place is known for its pies, and it has dozens of flavors. Each of us chose a favorite, and it was well worth the stop. If you like pie, you will definitely want to stop here. If you do not like pie, start liking pie and stop here for a piece.

We then headed north on Highway 89 and soon veered northwest on Route 17, also known as Chief Mountain International Highway.

After the road turned into Route 6, we hit the Canadian border. This choice had brought about one of the little extra costs of the trip. We had to obtain passports. The process can be a bit of a hassle, but once you have them, the passport cards are good for five to ten years for cruises and travel to Canada and Mexico. We crossed the border without incident and made our way to the park entrance as we turned southwest on Route 5. Alberta is known as Wild Rose Country, and as we wound our way to the hotel, we were right on the edge of a weather front. We left the sun for clouds and mist as we approached the historic Prince of Wales Hotel. This memorable place is at the base of Upper Waterton Lake, looking south into Glacier Park and a multitude of mountain peaks. We settled into our two rooms and set out to explore the alpine chalet-like hotel. It had been around almost ninety years, and it popped up prominently as I was researching park lodging before the trip. I felt it made the trip into Canada worth it. The rain intensified, so we relaxed in the Windsor lounge and in the great room, later enjoying dinner in the restaurant. I explored the grounds after the rain stopped, and the wind whipped strongly around the hotel corners. It was the middle of July, but it was definitely cold. As darkness ensued, we retreated to our quaint, comfortable rooms for the night.

Glacier National Park—Prince of Wales Hotel

We had breakfast by the front windows, watching as clouds and fog shrouded the mountains on either side of the lake. A short time later the sun finally won the battle, and we ventured out toward the cliffs and the water. We took pictures of the hotel, lake, boats, mountains, the town below us, our new biker friends, and one another. We then checked out and wound our way up Route 5. Instead of leaving the park, we turned west on Red Rock Parkway, heading up to a scenic area called Red Rock Canyon. I am assuming this is a pretty place to visit, but it unfortunately was closed to visitors when we got there. Nevertheless, the scenery on the way was pretty, and we even saw the butt of a grizzly bear about forty yards from the road as we were coming back. I stopped, but my wife did not let me get out of the car to take pictures. She mentioned mauling or something like that.

We were again on our way south, successfully making it back into the United States. A short time after we hit Highway 89 South, we took the Many Glacier entrance road back into the park. This took us through fields and trees along Lake Sherburne, and it ended at the Many Glacier Lodge. This was one of the places I had originally looked at to stay, but there were no vacancies. We checked it out, and it was really cool. We walked around the lobby and gift shop, and we strolled on the long, wide porch that ran along the side and front of the main building. This gave us spectacular views of the lake in front of us and the mountains and glacial snows across the water. We checked out trails in the hills above the hotel, exploring rapids, rocks, and plant life. Clouds covered some of the peaks while others were exposed to the sun. This was a beautiful area, and I hope to hike more of its trails in the future. Of course, everyone stops for any kind of wildlife, and we were fortunate enough to see a grizzled mountain goat make its way through the grounds. It stopped and seemed to pose for our pictures before it made its way into the forest. After our hike we made our way out of Many Glacier. We stopped a few more times for pictures, and we saw a moose not far away. We took pictures of fields of colorful wildflowers, sculpted mountains, and rushing water. Then we headed back out of the park.

Glacier National Park—Many Glacier Entrance

As we made our way south on Highway 89, we got back to the Saint Mary entrance to the Going to the Sun Road. Well, the Park Café called our names once again, so we stopped for pie. I had enjoyed the chocolate cream pie the day before, so I chose the banana cream pie this time. I was not disappointed. We continued south along the edge of the park, taking pictures from the car and loving the sunny scenery. We exited Highway 89 onto Route 49 South. This took us past the Two Medicine entrance to Glacier. Since it was getting later in the day, we skipped this one. However, given the lakes, mountains, waterfalls, and colorful rocks, I planned to return here someday. A short time later, we intersected with Highway 2 in East Glacier Park. This was our destination for the night, as we checked in to the Glacier Park Lodge. While it was not technically inside the park, it was a really cool place to stay. The huge pillars, support beams, and roofing frames were made out of large logs that gave it a distinctive look. There were multiple sections to the overall lodge, and we entered a fantastic great room to check in. This main room is one to be experienced. There are multiple levels, huge support logs, shops, restaurants, lounge areas, and the front desk. It is worth a stop, even if you are not staying there. There were excursions and trails from this lodge, but we opted to stay home and enjoy the sun at the pool. We wandered the grounds and took pictures of the mountains in the distance. We had dinner in the lodge restaurant, and I gave my wife and sons another present. I bought them massages near the teepee on the second floor of the main building. I also enjoyed another very tasty regional beer from the Big Sky Brewing Company. Their Trout Slayer Ale was quite refreshing. My wife also enjoyed their Summer Honey seasonal ale. Double yum. We slept like proverbial logs and prepared for our last day of trip fun.

Saturday morning was another beautiful day, and we spent time walking around the grounds of the Glacier Park Lodge, which is nicknamed "the Big Tree Hotel." The flowers, the railroad depot across the way, the structure, and the mountains in the park all combined to bring a rewarding close to our stay in and around Glacier. We had breakfast, relaxed on the fantastic balcony, and checked out. Our final stop was to be Missoula, but we chose to stick around the park a little while longer. The trip on Highway 2 around the southern edges of Glacier was very scenic. To our left were national forests, wilderness areas, the continental divide, creeks, and lakes. To our right was the beauty of Glacier National Park. It is no wonder this place has been called the "Crown of the Continent." Back at the west Glacier entrance, we decided to reenter the park and hit a few more turnouts near Lake McDonald. We got out and explored, enjoying the rocks, trees, rushing streams, and waterfalls under the nearly cloudless sky. We did manage to get separated for a while, and my younger son and I wandered a long distance along a stream, thinking my wife and other son were lost. It turns out we were lost. When we finally got back to the bridge by the turnout, they were there waiting for us. This brings up an important point about hiking, and someday I will figure out what it is.

Glacier National Park—West Glacier Turnout

Now it was time to head to Missoula. It was only a couple of hours away, and the day was perfect for travel. I chose Missoula as our fly back point because I have friends who live there. One of the sons of the family I grew up next to lives there with his family. They were the best neighbors I have ever had, and they made life on Wynes Street a lot more fun when I was a kid. I had contacted them earlier in the year, and we made plans to visit that Saturday in Missoula. The trip down Highways 2 and 93 to I-90 was easy, and we got to town midafternoon. We made our way through it and arrived at their house. We visited and reminisced, talking about our families and travels. It was relaxing, and they prepared the best meal of the trip for us. It was great to see them, and Missoula was a picturesque place to visit. We left near dusk and made our way to the Days Inn for our final night. The flight was very early Sunday morning, but we were very close to the airport. We relaxed Saturday night and flew home the next day. The flights took us to Denver and then to Pittsburgh, and we were home once again after a fabulous week in the Northwest.

SUMMATION

The northern areas of the West provided new adventures and different kinds of awesome sights than where we had been on prior trips. This excursion was a lot of fun to plan and even more fun to experience. The many climates and terrains offered us a variety of natural wonders, and the sheer beauty of it all gave us perhaps the best trip ever! *A week in Olympic National Park, Glacier National Park, Waterton Park in Canada, Mount St. Helens National Volcanic Monument, and a wonderful drive along I-90 provided one of the greatest family adventures yet.* This also made me want to return to each park, as there were still many places within them that I wanted to see. The daylong trip to Mount St. Helens was awesome, but it did take most of a day away from us in Olympic. We did not get to experience the wonders of the Hoh Rain Forest or the Sol Duc Hot Springs. There are numerous places in the northwest section of the park that I would have loved to have seen, including Ozette, Pillar Point, Shi Shi Beach, Point of the Arches, and Neah Bay. The eastern side of Olympic has Dosewallips, Seal Rock, and the Dungeness area among many others. This unique peninsula could easily be afforded a week itself, but our days there were filled with an abundance of memorable places and activities. Glacier, like Olympic, has scores of incredible hiking trails within its interior, and the next time we go, these will be on the docket as much as possible. There are limitations to travel in these parks depending on the time of year, so our July visit worked out very well. We did endure some rain, but it was all part of the natural beauty. The parks as well as the natural splendor of Washington, Idaho, and Montana gave us an unforgettable experience.

Family at a Glacier National Park Waterfall

Spend as much time as you can in each of these places because as far as national parks go, they are at the top of the list. In previous chapters I have generally included one picture for each place visited. Olympic and Glacier are more like four or five places in one, so each park has numerous pictures. I hope you like them. I also spent more on this trip, as lodging, activities, and the rental car were higher than usual (but worth it to me). After three trips out west, we had seen so many incredible places that I was running out of superlatives to assign to them. However, I would have to come up with some more, because we were not done yet.

CHAPTER 5: WESTERN ODYSSEY #4
CALIFORNIA, HERE WE COME (2012)

PREPARATIONS

The year 2011 was another break year, as I was accumulating airline miles. The summer was also extremely busy with sports, goalie camps, theater, fitness classes, Space Camp, home remodeling, and parts in the Batman movie *The Dark Knight Rises*. I was the one in the yellow jacket at the top of the stadium during the football scene. My big trip of the year involved taking my parents back home to Michigan for a week in July to visit family and friends. My small trip was a weekend Florida smooth jazz cruise with my wife that February. The year 2011 also gave me an opportunity to start planning for our next Western Odyssey. Because my older son was graduating from high school, 2012 would be a milestone year for us. He was staying home for his last summer before college, and I wanted to continue our western excursions as long as possible. We had been to many of the national park heavyweights in the western lower forty-eight, but there was still one really big one we had not been to or driven through—Yosemite National Park. California also has many more parks and places to experience, and standing between Las Vegas and Yosemite is Death Valley National Park. With each trip I have tried to not duplicate any prior destinations aside from Las Vegas. However, I also had wanted to go back to Zion National Park to hike the Narrows ever since our brief 2006 introduction. Thus, it was added to the mix. During the planning of this fabulous montage, we had been watching a cable weather show where an Australian photographer would go to scenic places to get the perfect picture. It was interesting because he went to a number of places we had already been to, and it was nice to relive them and see his great photographs. I wish mine were like that. One of the places he went to was a slot canyon near Lake Powell, Arizona, called Upper Antelope Canyon. I give the bloke credit for demonstrating its allure, as we added this to our trip itinerary. I knew we would not get many more chances to take trips like this, so I wanted this experience to be really memorable.

Step one was choosing when we would go. Like prior years, we had many priorities and activities to plan. Our younger son was taking driver's training classes, and we were planning a high school graduation party for our older son. We decided to have the party on the first Friday in July and then leave that weekend for an extended trip. This time we would be gone nearly ten full days. It would be our longest trip yet. We chose Sunday, July 8, as our departure date, and we would continue through the following weekend and beyond.

Step two was figuring out how we would get there from Pennsylvania. Again, by the end of 2011, I had amassed enough miles on my credit card to fly us west for free. We decided to use Las Vegas as our hub, flying into McCarran International Airport and returning from there. The flight out would be at 5:35 a.m. on Sunday, giving us all day to travel and sightsee with the time change. The return flight would be the afternoon of Tuesday, July 17. I booked the flights in January and started working on lodging soon after that.

Step three was determining where we were going to visit and on what days. Our friends from Southern California were able to rendezvous with us the second weekend, so we could spend a few days together. We would arrive in Las Vegas early Sunday, July 8, and the drive to Death Valley was only a few hours. This would give us a lot of daylight to explore some of the wonders of the park. Monday morning would be our drive to Yosemite, so we would have some time to check out the northern areas of Death Valley and experience the rural heart of California as we headed north. Tuesday and Wednesday would be spent in Yosemite, and Thursday would be the big driving day all the way to Zion in Utah. Friday would be spent in Zion, and Saturday morning would take us to Hurricane, Utah, and off-roading in the mountains. We would then travel later that day to Lake Powell near Page, Arizona, spending the night and all day Sunday there. We would enjoy jet skis on the lake and a tour of Upper Antelope Canyon. Monday would take us back to Las Vegas and a relaxing finale at the pool. So the trip route was set—Death Valley National Park, Yosemite National Park, Zion National Park, off-roading in Warner Valley, Lake Powell in the Glen Canyon National Recreation Area, Upper Antelope Canyon, and the Beach at Mandalay Bay Resort in Las Vegas. This was going to be a lot of fun.

Step four was determining where we were going to stay each night. In early March, I worked to secure all lodging so we would not have any problems. Xanterra was still the organization handling lodging reservations in Zion and in Death Valley. The premier lodging sites in Yosemite included the Ahwahnee Hotel, Curry Village, and the Yosemite Lodge at the Falls. At this point only Curry Village had available vacancies. It is recommended that you book Yosemite lodging well in advance. Using online booking sites, the best-looking place in the Lake Powell area was the Lake Powell Resort and Marina itself. For our final night the Mandalay Bay had plenty of rooms. I hesitated with picking Curry Village, and within a couple of days it had filled up. So I researched lodging near the park, and I found Yosemite's Four Seasons Vacation Rentals. I found a loft condo in Yosemite West that was about fifteen miles south of the Yosemite Valley, and it worked out very well. So the plan was this—Furnace Creek Resort in Death Valley on Sunday night; Yosemite West Condo on Monday, Tuesday, and Wednesday nights; Zion Park Lodge on Thursday and Friday nights; Lake Powell Resort on Saturday and Sunday nights; and Mandalay Bay in Las Vegas for our final night.

Step five was adding tours and additional activities on to the location visits. Like Yellowstone, Yosemite offered an all-day bus tour. I booked this for Tuesday morning. For Saturday I reserved UTV side-by-side off-road vehicles to drive in Warner Valley outside of Hurricane, Utah. For Sunday we reserved jet skis for an adventure on Lake Powell.

Step six was choosing certain meals to get a little fancy with. This time around I was not sure where we would be each night, so I did not reserve any specific meals. I figured we would have enough choices wherever we were. I still budgeted accordingly based on an estimated amount each day.

Step seven was choosing what vehicle we would drive around in. I originally wanted to go off-roading in southern Utah, so I looked at a good all-wheel-drive vehicle. After I reserved the side-by-sides for off-road fun, I changed to something a little more practical. I chose a minivan.

Step eight was making sure we had the right supplies. The adult Merrells were still working for us, so the boys had to find comfortable shoes. We did not have a lot of extensive hiking planned, so we were in good shape. Hot weather clothing, sunscreen, hats, sunglasses, electronics, etc., were all part of the packing. We would pick up anything else we needed on the trip. We also employed GPS for this trip to enhance our mapping capabilities.

Step nine was budgeting for the 2012 Nevada-California-Nevada-Utah-Nevada trip. The following worksheet is adapted from the spreadsheet file I use for all of our major trips. It shows the plans for the schedule, locations, activities, estimated costs and miles, actual costs, and the timing of the payments for each item.

2012 TRAVEL COSTS FOR OUR FUN						
DATES	DESTINATION	ITEM	ESTIMATES	PAID	DATES	MILES
07/12	West swing IV	Flights — add'l costs	40.00	40.00	1/19/2012	
07/12	West swing IV	Lodging — Furnace Creek	169.12	0.00	3/06/2012	—
07/12	West swing IV	Lodging — Yosemite — Four Seasons Condos	397.38	397.38	3/06/2012	350
07/12	West swing IV	Lodging — Yosemite — Four Seasons Condos	198.69	198.69	6/24/2012	155
07/12	West swing IV	Lodging — Zion Park Lodge	193.24	193.24	3/06/2012	660
07/12	West swing IV	Lodging — Zion Park Lodge	193.24	193.24	7/14/2012	
07/12	West swing IV	Lodging — Lake Powell Resort (2 nights)	363.90	363.90	3/06/2012	150
07/12	West swing IV	Lodging — Mandalay Bay Hotel	184.80	184.80	3/07/2012	280
07/12	West swing IV	Lodging — Luxor (Replacement)		50.40	7/08/2012	
07/12	West swing IV	Jet Skis	500.00	635.95	7/15/2012	
07/12	West swing IV	UTVs	600.00	614.13	7/14/2012	
07/12	West swing IV	Bus Tour	328.00	328.00	6/15/2012	
07/12	West swing IV	Rental Car	311.00	314.33	7/17/2012	
07/12	West swing IV	Antelope Canyon	0.00	280.00	7/15/2012	
07/12	West swing IV	Miles Estimate — 1,900				
07/12	West swing IV	Park Fees — Annual Pass	80.00	95.00	7/09/2012	
07/12	West swing IV	Flights — add'l costs	0.00	57.00	7/17/2012	
07/12	West swing IV	Meals estimate 07/08-07/17 (est. $100/day)	900.00	1,102.62	7/12	
07/12	West swing IV	Misc. Food	200.00	0.00	7/12	
07/12	West swing IV	Misc., Nick Knacks, Shirts	200.00	197.10	7/12	
07/12	West swing IV	Gas (estimate 23 mpg x $4 x total estimated miles)	330.43	181.61	7/12	
07/12	West swing IV	Cash — Initial	350.00	350.00		
07/12	West swing IV	Cash — ATMs on trip	0.00			
07/12	West swing IV	Parking —Airport 07/17/12 (9 days)	72.00	80.00	7/17/2012	
Aug Visa	3,801.38	Totals	$5,611.80	$5,857.39		1,595
Pre-	1,706.01					
Cash	350.00					
	5,857.39					

THE TRIP!

I was not sure how many more family trips we would be able to take in the future, so I wanted to pack as much into this one as I could. Using extensive online research, I armed myself with maps and information about the places we would visit. I was excited about our lodging choices, even though we were not actually inside Yosemite Valley this time. This was going to be a fun and rewarding adventure out west. We cleaned up after my son's graduation party, packed on Saturday, and flew out at 5:30 a.m. on Sunday, July 8. Getting to the airport with enough time can be stressful, and we actually hit a traffic jam going through Pittsburgh at three in the morning. Who would have thought it? Fortunately we made it in time, and we prepared for the first leg of our flight that would take us to Dulles Airport in Washington, DC. *This is when the trip changed abruptly.* The flight was short, but as we started our initial descent, my older son started panicking. He was just across the aisle from me, and he was in massive pain. The flight attendant worked to comfort him, but the pain was so sharp I could feel it myself. I felt like Rick watching Carl helplessly early in season two of *The Walking Dead*. We landed, and the emergency medical technicians were waiting for us. As a precaution, we all rode to the Reston Hospital in an ambulance, taking our carry-ons with us. My son had stabilized, and the diagnosis was that the conditions caused acute sinus pressure issues. The altitude changes exacerbated it and caused him major discomfort and pain. We stayed for a while, and then a cab took us to pick up prescription narcotics and decongestants before we headed back to Dulles. We were thankful he was okay, but we had to deal with the reality that we had missed our morning flight to Las Vegas.

I knew people who had visited Death Valley, and I really wanted to witness its unique features. The park was only a couple of hours from Vegas, so we would have had most of Sunday and some of Monday morning to explore it. The Badwater and Furnace Creek areas seemed to offer us the most bang for the buck. Scratch all that. The airline was very helpful and got us on another flight to Vegas later that day, but we were in for a long eight-hour wait at the airport. This would get us to Vegas around ten that night. So I got online and started revamping. Death

Valley was lost to us, so I contacted the Furnace Creek Resort to see if they would refund my room cost. They were very accommodating and did so because of the details of the situation. When I do end up going to Death Valley—and I will—my lodging of choice will be Furnace Creek. I also had to find a room for the night in Vegas. I chose the Luxor, as it was close to the airport and we had stayed there before. Everything was set, so the only other inconvenience was that the Monday drive to Yosemite would be quite a bit longer than we had originally planned. This was not a big deal, and we were back on track with a modified best trip ever!

We did have one more thing to do Monday morning after we checked out of the Luxor and got on the road. We had chosen to rent a minivan late Sunday, and we took it back to the hotel. I quickly realized that it was not the kind of vehicle we were used to. We exchanged it for a midsize SUV that morning, and we were on our way. Our goal was to enter Yosemite at the northeast entrance near Lee Vining, California, approximately 350 miles away. After a few quick jaunts on I-215 and I-15 out of Vegas, we hit NV-160 to the northwest through Pahrump. Since we were bypassing Death Valley, much of the drive would be fairly open with a lot of desertlike scenery. Soon we turned onto US-95, and we eventually headed west on NV-266. This would take us into California from Nevada, and it would slow us down somewhat. However, it took us through beautiful mountains and forests as it turned into Highway CA-168, so the scenery gave us more variety. We popped into a valley and turned north near Big Pine onto US-395. This took us through towns like Bishop, Tom's Place, Mammoth Lakes, and June Lake Junction as we gained altitude. Just before Lee Vining, we turned west onto Highway 120. This road took us into Yosemite as it became Tioga Pass Road. We were still nearly ninety park miles from our room. According to the National Park Service, this road is closed from November through May, so I was happy we were able to experience it. Just before the park entrance, we passed Tioga Peak, which is more than eleven thousand feet high.

We picked up a copy of the park newspaper *Yosemite Guide* at the entrance. Our plans for the next few days did not include specific time to explore this northern section, so I am glad we took this route. It allowed us to at least see the beauty of the Yosemite wilderness in this part of the park. We passed lakes, numerous domes, peaks with snow pockets, dense forests, and Tuolumne Meadows. It was a gorgeous drive on a fun, curvy road. There were many places to stop and wander the high country. However, it was late in the day, and the shadows were heavy across the road. We wanted to get dinner and pick up some supplies, so we stopped at the White Wolf turnout. Unfortunately we were too late to get food, but the nice lady there told us Yosemite newbies that the Yosemite Lodge at the Falls had restaurant and grocery services open until at least nine. We hit the road and continued west, finally turning east toward the Yosemite Valley on Highway 140. It was dusk, but the entrance into Yosemite Valley was awesome. We drove along the Merced River, passing El Capitan and other majestic granite mountains. We got to the lodge just in time, and we were able to get groceries at the General Store and enjoy a great meal in the Mountain Room Restaurant. It was dark when we left, but we found our way to our Yosemite West condo in the southern section of the park. We settled in and rested up for the big tour on Tuesday.

The Yosemite Grand Tour is an all-day bus tour through the park, taking you to many of the highlight locations in and around Yosemite Valley. We drove the winding road north into the valley, and we had a terrific view as the sun was peaking over the mountains. We met at the Yosemite Lodge, boarding the bus just before nine. Our guide was knowledgeable and friendly, and she made a short stop in the valley to let us gaze at climbers high on a rock facing above us. I think she was kidding, as I never actually saw the climbers. She also reminded us not to leave any food in our vehicles, particularly after dark, as curious bears could sense it. We then made our way south to Glacier Point Road. This winding, scenic route is also closed during the winter. Our guide told us stories of this place as we rode on. After a period of time we ended up high above the Yosemite Valley, where we had started the tour. We walked the maintained trails, climbing rocks and finding a multitude of photo opportunities. Half Dome, the Merced River, valley forests, mountains, and waterfalls presented view after view of continuous beauty. We stayed at Glacier Point for a while and then departed on the bus. The winding road took us back to Wawona Road, where we turned south. We made our way to the Wawona Hotel, stopping for lunch. This was a really cool structure with a fountain in the large courtyard, creeks, stables, a bridge, and a golf course. We did not tee off, but we grabbed a snack in the pro shop. This gave us a nice break before we headed south again to the Mariposa Grove of Giant Sequoias.

Yosemite National Park—Glacier Point

The big trees are near the south entrance to Yosemite, and we got off the bus and onto several large tram cars for the tree tour. We weaved through the forest, and our guide told stories of the trees and the associated human history. Whether standing or fallen, the sequoias were huge and prominent. Many of them had names, and some had been carved out at the base to allow people and cars to pass through their trunks. We took turns riding and walking trails, checking out a small museum and exploring the magnificent trees before departing. The bus ride back to the lodge had one more signature stop to make at the Tunnel View turnout. Right after Wawona Road turns east and takes you through a tunnel, you exit to a point high above Yosemite Valley. Tunnel View gives you a fantastic view of the forest below and the valley in the distance. El Capitan on the left, Bridalveil Fall on the right, Half Dome in the distance, and the valley in the middle all combined to put an exclamation point on the tour. I recommend visiting this spot at different times of the day to enjoy the sights from different perspectives and with different lighting.

Yosemite National Park—Giant Sequoia Trees

We finished our sightseeing and headed back on the bus to the lodge. It was near dinnertime, so we hit one of our favorite spots in the park. The Yosemite Lodge food court was a very convenient place that we used numerous times. After we ate, we ventured a little east in the valley, stopping to check out the historic Ahwahnee Hotel. This was a really beautiful place in a great location, and we wandered around for a while, inside and out. I checked out the restaurant, and I found they offered an interesting sounding meal of nuts, berries, and cheese. We took some pictures and enjoyed the beauty before we headed back to our condo near dusk.

The next morning we had no specific plans, but we wanted to hike in Yosemite. That was put on hold temporarily, as we found that our battery had died during the night. It was probably because I was out in the vehicle the night before, connecting to Wi-Fi and checking things back at the office. Let this be a lesson to you. Vacation is for vacation, not work. Fortunately there were some construction workers nearby, and they were able to jump-start us. We headed back north to the valley, stopping briefly again at Tunnel View to take some more pictures and prepare for fun on the trails. We headed into the valley for some hiking and water activities. Our first stop was Bridalveil Fall. A short paved trail took us to the rocky terrain under the waterfall, and we took pictures and marveled at the colors and wind-affected water. We had also thought about a raft trip on the Merced, so we drove to Curry Village, where the rentals were located. After some discussion we decided to forego rafting.

Yosemite National Park—Tunnel View

We parked at the Yosemite Lodge again and made sure our water bottles were filled. Across from the lodge was the Lower Yosemite Fall Trail. We strolled through tall trees on the well-maintained trails, and we crossed a wooden bridge and jumped into some real fun. Earlier in the year I had torn part of the meniscus in my left knee, so I was somewhat concerned about this kind of hiking. Fortunately my regimen of self-healing by lying around a lot helped enough to allow me to hike nearly pain-free. A rocky slope led us up to the mountainside where the waterfall was on the right and climbers were on the left. We climbed over rocks from a few feet in diameter to some taller than we were. There were trees, plants, dirt, and rocks giving us choices on where and how we wanted to ascend. This was a lot of fun, and it took us up to a large pool under the cascading waterfall. People were swimming and lying under the spray.

Yosemite National Park—Lower Yosemite Falls

We got right next to the falling water and cooled ourselves in the smaller pools between the rocks all around us. From different vantage points we could see Half Dome, rock climbers, and trees back in the valley. The climbing offered a physical workout in addition to the beauty. We did not make the longer hike to Upper Yosemite Fall, but we spent a lot of quality time in the cool watery Lower Fall area. The hike down was an opportunity to find different routes to make the descent easier. We headed back to the lodge to relax a little. Since we did not go rafting, we chose to make another stop in the valley. We found one of the many access trails to the Merced River and prepared for our own water excursion. We waded across the Merced to the bank on the other side. I took pictures and watched our stuff as my wife and the boys waded and swam upstream toward a large rock in the river. They climbed it and jumped off, enjoying the refreshing water. After our river fun we dried off and headed back into the valley interior. We stopped again and walked over bridges and into the meadows, taking pictures and taking in the views one last time. The views of Half Dome as the sun was setting were pretty incredible. It was getting close to dusk when we left the valley. We stopped at the Lodge for more supplies and headed back to the condo. One of the supplies I was fortunate to procure was a package of the Mammoth Brewing Company's Ahwahnee Amber Ale. This was a delicious representative of the many beers of Northern California. (I believe their amber ale has since been renamed.)

Our time at Yosemite was only a few days, but we experienced the inspiring splendor of the park in many ways. More than 90 percent of the park is wilderness, and it offers everything you might want in a place like this. I do wish we had gotten to the Vernal Fall and Nevada Fall trails in the eastern part of the valley, but they give me more to see when I return. The northern section of the park, including the Hetch Hetchy and Tuolumne Meadows areas, will also be on my list for the future. The granite mountains, numerous bodies of water, rewarding hikes, flowing meadows, and breathtaking views are excellent reasons to plan a Yosemite adventure. The National Park Service brochure offers a lot of useful information, and one tidbit explains what to do in case a mountain lion attacks. It says to look large and fight back. Fortunately we did not see any mountain lions, but I was ready for them. Moreover, there was a small issue with Hantavirus in Curry Village the exact time we were looking to stay there in 2012. While the rodent-borne illness was absolutely no fault of theirs, it makes for an interesting little side story about the coincidence and our good fortune.

Thursday was the really big driving day. We would not be returning via the route we had taken to get to the park. There were a number of alternate routes we could have taken, but I chose to drive southeast through the heart of California and back through Las Vegas on the way to Zion National Park in southern Utah. The car started for us, and we packed up, checked out, and hit the road. We made our way toward the park and turned down Highway CA-41 (Wawona Road) toward the south entrance of Yosemite. We were descending for about an hour, turning southeast on CA-99 outside of Fresno. It was just more than one hundred miles through numerous small towns to Bakersfield. We were thinking about some lunch, and I decided we would stop after Bakersfield. Bad idea. We turned on CA-58 and headed through mountains and rolling fields of gold, but there were very few towns or facilities on this stretch. It was a beautiful drive, and fortunately the town of Tehachapi finally appeared. We stopped for food and gas, and we were on our way again. We passed Mojave and the huge Edwards Air Force Base site. This was really cool to see. Near Barstow, we turned northeast on I-15. Much of the drive through the middle of California included vineyards and different food crops as far as the eye could see. Soon we were in the desert, where flora and fauna were replaced by sand, sagebrush, and cacti. We cranked the speed and blew through Las Vegas on our way to Zion. More interesting sights were in store as we passed through the smoke of wildfires near the Nevada border. We could also see the rain north of us, driving through occasional cloudbursts as the sunlight was waning to our west. We passed through the scenic northwest corner of Arizona and through St. George, Utah, turning east on Highway 9. As we drove through Hurricane past dusk, the rain intensified, and we were hoping the next couple of days would not be washouts. Since we were staying at the Zion Park Lodge, we were able to drive right into the park and up to the lodge. We checked in and had a late dinner at the lodge restaurant. We rested up for our Friday hike.

I have tried to always do new things each vacation, but this was our second trip to Zion. However, the first time in 2006 was a short jaunt, and we did not get into the Narrows. That was the main goal this time around. Armed with the park map and wilderness guides, we set out to reacquaint ourselves with the place. It was still overcast that morning when we walked across the Zion park road to the lower emerald pools trail. We took some pictures and headed back to the shuttle stop. We took it up to the Weeping Rock trail, hiking to the natural water dripper as it sprinkled outside. We got back on the shuttle and decided to just ride for a while. It took us to the end of the road and all the way back out of the main park to the visitor center. At least it wasn't pouring like the night before. Flash flooding was discussed as a remote possibility, but the Narrows had not yet been closed to hikers. The shuttle took us back onto the park road, and as we hit each stop, something great started happening. The sky began to clear, and the sun was coming out. We decided we were prepped for the water, so we rode up to the end of the park loop road and the Temple of Sinawava, which is also called the "Gateway to the Narrows." We hit the restrooms, filled our water bottles, and headed up the mile-long river walk trail to the Narrows. We stopped to take pictures of many of the rock formations and reenact poses from six years earlier. Of course, the boys were much bigger now. There were rocks to climb on, and critters crossed our path as we trekked to the end of the walkway. When we got there shortly after noon, we knew this was our time to hike the Narrows.

We walked down the steps to the edge of the Virgin River and started across the first section. There were sturdy walking sticks available near the water's edge on a use-and-return honor system, but we left them for other hikers. Much of the bottom was covered by rounded rocks, which I have seen described as slippery bowling balls. Thus, we wore our hiking shoes right into the water. My older son carried the backpack with our supplies, and I had the cameras. The deepest the water would get for us was near the start. We crossed from one bank to another through waist-high water, wary of the current and the slick river bottom. As you progress into the Narrows, you are often between very high walls where shadows are prevalent and breezes blow. Fortunately the sun was high in the sky, and the clouds were breaking up. The heat made it very refreshing to be in the water, and we enjoyed small pools, light rapids, and waterfalls as we made our way in. There were sandy shores, rocky shores, sections with no shores, hills, trees, and rocks all within the high Navajo sandstone walls of this magnificent canyon.

Zion National Park—The Narrows

The water current fluctuated as we moved up the canyon, ranging from rushing rapids to still pools. The whole Narrows hike is approximately sixteen miles long, but you can only go about halfway up before you need a permit, equipment, and even a guide. My goal was to go as far as we could before we had to turn around. Orderville Canyon is a tributary creek that branches off several hours upstream, so that seemed like a reasonable goal. We continued our journey over the varied terrain, twisting through canyon turns to see what would come up next. This was an extraordinary place, and I took many pictures to try to record our first time in this part of the park. We hiked for a few hours before we finally decided to turn around and make our way back. What seemed like a very long distance was probably not more than a couple of miles, and we definitely did not make Orderville Canyon. Nevertheless, it was an exhilarating venture into one of the most famous slot canyons in the southwest. The return trip was much quicker, and our shoes squished repeatedly as we made our way back to the shuttle stop. We went where we had not gone before, and maybe someday we would go in even farther.

The hike was pretty tiring, so we changed and relaxed in the room. Of course, we were all hungry, and it was dinnertime. Not far outside of the park was the town of Springdale, Utah. We decided to drive out and find someplace to eat there. We found Casa De Amigos on the main street, and we were rewarded with a great meal. The sun played more peekaboo, and we experienced some sprinkles as night made its entrance. The next day would bring more activities, so we retired to our room at the lodge. Our second trip to Zion was even more fun than the first, and I secretly planned to return again someday.

We had planned our off-roading adventure for Saturday morning, so we checked out of the lodge and headed out. It was still overcast and drizzling in the park, but the sun came out after we exited. Not far from Zion is the town of Hurricane, and the Southern Utah Adventure Center is the big dog in town when it comes to outdoor fun. They rent all kinds of water and land vehicles for half days, full days, and more. After extensive research I contacted them in April and reserved two of their Polaris RZR UTVs (utility terrain vehicles) for our July escapade. These side-by-sides are very durable and feature full roll cages for the occupants. If you have driven these before, you know how much fun they are. If you have not, find a way to get out and do it. There are many places in southern Utah to enjoy, and the owner suggested I take advantage of the combination of Warner Valley and Sand Mountain. These were directly accessible from the SUAC shop after a short ride through town. We were originally going to go out ourselves, but we were thankfully convinced to take a guide. I am pretty certain I would have gotten lost.

After it rains here, it generally dries up quickly, and the trails kick up a lot of dust. However, the owner told us that the recent rainfall was more than usual, so it was possible we might encounter some standing water. We loaded a cooler with waters and snacks, and the three vehicles set off toward the valley. We hit the dirt trails into the valley surrounded by colorful mountains, mesas, and hills. Some trail sections had large dips. These were easily navigable by the UTVs, but the hard ground gave the water no place to go but up. Not long into the trip, we found the trail water. It did not matter if we went through it fast or slow. We got swamped multiple times. We were covered with orange muddy water, and the UTVs were caked in mud. In any case, this was fun. The bright side was that the dust was minimized, even as the temperature approached 100 degrees. My white T-shirt and hat were forever changed with orange spots everywhere. We found the moon mounds and hit these purple hills hard. Climbs, jumps, hairpins, washes, and slots gave us a great feel for what we could do in the UTVs. We continued along the trails, driving at varied speeds over rocks, moguls, dips, bumps, winding curves, and more water.

We stopped for a break and checked out the dinosaur tracks etched into stone along a section of the valley. While we were there, I photographed a lizard, a horny toad, and my muddy family. We continued on, weaving through ravines, climbing over rocks, and accelerating through straightaways. We eventually four-wheeled to a higher elevation where we encountered massive sand dunes above the Sand Hollow Reservoir.

07/14/2012

Hurricane, Utah—UTV Side by Sides in Warner Valley

The mud was gone, but we were in for more fun as we hit the hills and made patterns all over the sand. The UTVs plowed through the dunes, and we had beautiful views of the valley behind us and the reservoir in front of us. My older son was the smartest of us as he donned a bandana to block the debris from his mouth. I was too busy picking sand out of my teeth. We switched drivers multiple times, and everyone got a chance to drive on different terrains. Sometime before our tour was to end, the thunderstorms we had been watching in the distance edged closer. Occasional flashes told us that we were nearing the end of the romp. We made our way out of the dunes and down to the highway where our final leg would take us back to the SUAC. We switched into two-wheel drive and took turns falling back and then briefly speeding up to near sixty miles per hour. We stopped at a car wash to clean the mud off the UTVs, and this was no small undertaking. When we got back to the shop, we knew we had a three-hour drive to Lake Powell, so the owner did us an extraordinary favor by allowing us to change clothes and try to get the mud off in the garage. We thanked him and our guide for the memorable day on the trails. This was something I definitely wanted to do again someday.

After a quick lunch we left Hurricane for Lake Powell near Page, Arizona. We continued east on Highway 9 back toward Zion National Park. I had wanted to go to another spot where we had not been before. We passed the main canyon entrance and headed through the southeast part of the park, winding our way toward the mile-long Zion-Mount Carmel Tunnel. We passed more Navajo sandstone mountain faces, rounded mesas, and tree-dotted rock formations. This is part of Scenic Byway 9, and it is definitely worth the drive. We came out into the clear and eventually turned onto US-89, turning south and then east and then south again to the Lake Powell Resort across the dam from Page. On the way we caught up with the rain and went through some really cool desert storms. You could see them develop over the mesas in the distance, and you would finally drive through the downpour. Fortunately the rain stayed north, and we got to the resort near dinnertime. We had been to the Glen Canyon National Recreation Area in 2008, but that raft trip was on the river below the dam. This time we were above it on the lake. We met up with our California friends, and after we settled into our rooms, the eight of us drove into Page. We found an Italian restaurant and enjoyed warm evening breezes as we ate outside. After we returned to our rooms, we enjoyed the beautiful views of Lake Powell, the mesas and islands in the distance, and Wahweap Marina. We wandered around the compound and did some stargazing after dark. We relaxed and prepared for a busy Sunday.

Upper Antelope Canyon near Page, Arizona

After we determined that everyone wanted to ride jet skis Sunday morning, we rented four water craft from the Wahweap Marina down the road from the resort. We were on our own on the lake, and we headed out toward the dam. The lake was fairly rough in places, so we could feel a lot of the bumps. We suffered one setback, as my two strapping boys were unfortunately given what was later described as "one of the less stable jet skis we have for rent." They became unbalanced and capsized their craft. I had to get in the water before I planned to, and we switched groups after I struggled to get it back upright. Now I was with my younger son. We spent the next several hours hitting the waves at high speeds, slaloming through channels, exploring openings in the rocks, and beaching our jet skis on multiple beaches. The day was perfect, and we enjoyed the views all around the lake. Not long after noon we made our way back to the docks and headed back to the rooms to get ready for our afternoon slot canyon tour. I had reserved our spots for the four-thirty Upper Antelope Canyon tour with the Antelope Canyon Tours Company in Page.

We drove into Page and readied ourselves at the location on Lake Powell Boulevard. We piled into the back of a large four-wheel-drive truck with other tourists, sitting on the long, padded benches. We drove through town and then into a sandy canyon, making our way to the natural wonder they described as a "spectacular petrified sand dune, created by wind, water and sand, presenting a sculptured masterpiece." They hit it right on the head. Our group disembarked and followed the guide through the canyon. We walked along the sand floor of the slot canyon, weaving through magnificent shapes, patterns, and colors. Since we were on the final tour of the day, the sun was well behind the walls, and we went through some small sections that were nearly pitch black. I took picture after picture, realizing the Australian guy on the cable weather show was a much better photographer than me. We made our way several hundred yards through the canyon and out the other side, and we rested for a few minutes before we headed back the way we came. The canyon is not huge, and tour is not long; however, the beauty is breathtaking. I think a tour earlier in the day would provide better overall colors and views, but this was awesome nonetheless. I recommend a steady hand or a tripod to get some of the pictures, as shutter speed and lack of motion will help with photography inside the canyon. After we got back to the entrance, we meandered back to the truck, waiting for the guide. I decided to head back into the slot canyon again to see it in a different light and take more pictures. I am glad I did, as I captured even more fantastic memories. As we made our way back to the tour shop, the rain approached. We found a great place to eat while it poured outside. We had dinner at the Dam Bar and Grille in Page, enjoying their cuisine and a couple of Damber draft beers. The rain passed as we ate, and we headed back to the resort, basking in our great day. Another great sight I had wanted to see near Page was Horseshoe Bend, but we ran out of time and enthusiasm. It is on the list for next time.

07/16/2012

Lake Powell above Glen Canyon Dam

We had just a little less than three hundred miles to drive to Las Vegas on Monday, so after we checked out, we hit US-89 and made it to Kanab, Utah, in time for lunch. We stopped at a great little drive-in for burgers and headed south on US-89A, turning west on Arizona Highway 389. We passed Colorado City and crossed back into Utah, where the road became Highway 59. Through this stretch we witnessed more desert storms, and they were really cool to watch materialize. At Hurricane we turned onto Highway 9 and took it to I-15, stopping at our favorite Dairy Queen for ice cream on the way. From there we went through St. George, the beautiful northwest corner of Arizona, Mesquite, Nevada, and the open desert, on our way to the Mandalay Bay Resort on the south end of the Strip. After we checked in, we hit the sandy beach at the Mandalay Bay pool to enjoy the 100 degree afternoon. It was awesome and a tremendous way to put an exclamation point on another fantastic western odyssey. We had dinner at the Mandalay Bay buffet, where I think I ate more at one meal than I ever had in my life. We wandered through the connected hotels and even found a store where the Australian guy had his photographs displayed. Yup, my pictures sucked compared to his. After another great day we retired to the hotel room to rest before the Tuesday flight home.

We had some breakfast with our friends and said good-bye Tuesday morning. The only travel drama left came from the airline. There were issues with our flight, but fortunately they had a slightly earlier flight that we could take. Instead of a layover in Chicago, we had one in Charlotte. We quickly headed to the airport, dropped off our rental car, and made it through security in time. We got home that night, relieved to be home but still talking about the tremendous fun we had had out west.

SUMMATION

Fantastic, extraordinary, breathtaking, amazing—I can keep going, but you get the picture. Another western excursion had been envisioned, planned for, taken, and enjoyed. We dealt with a Death Valley curve ball in the first few hours of the trip, but we improvised and experienced incredible sights and activities throughout our time on this trip—Las Vegas, Yosemite National Park, central California, Zion National Park and the Narrows, Lake Powell and the Glen Canyon National Recreation Area, Upper Antelope Canyon, and a sandy beach at Mandalay Bay. This easily ranks as one of the *best trips Ever!* The weather cooperated with us, and some rain even afforded us experiences we normally would not have had. I recommend this trip in whole or a permutation, as it was really fun. We stayed in some very nice and convenient lodging, and the rental car was much cheaper because we returned back to Vegas. Renting the UTVs and jet skis was not inexpensive, but these were both memorable activities that led to a desire to do them again here or back home. Research the parks, pick the trails and activities, and get there whenever you can. Since my son had just graduated, this may have been the last western odyssey for a long time. However, I would keep planning just in case. There were still places to see and some unfinished business.

07/14/2012

Family after Muddy UTV Fun in Hurricane, Utah

CHAPTER 6: WESTERN ODYSSEY #5
SOMETHING OLD, SOMETHING NEW (2014)

PREPARATIONS

The year 2013 was another year without an odyssey. We managed to get a little family away time as we picked up my older son from college in Florida and took a weekend Bahama cruise in early May. That summer our college sophomore traveled to Virginia to compete in a UAV competition, and the high school junior totaled his first car a month after he got it. We got heavier into ice hockey. I took my parents back home to Michigan again, and we attended a tenth anniversary celebration for a Washington-based wounded troop charity we had been involved with since 2006. We were all very busy, and as the future began to take shape, it looked like we would have to forego the next installment of our biannual western odysseys.

The year 2014 would become a year of big change and big events, but I would keep a trip in the back of my mind just in case. My younger son took us to Canada and a memorable hockey tournament, and he starred as Donkey in *Shrek the Musical*, bringing down the house with his performance. My older son decided to stay in Florida for the summer after he landed a UAV internship and a job at Hooters (cook, not waiter). My wife renewed her status as a fitness instructor after a two-year hiatus, and the company where I had worked for more than fifteen years decided (without explanation) to eliminate my position as of the end of June. Summer was going to be different in many ways. It was early May when I decided to make an old idea a reality. I had often discussed our family vacations with friends and colleagues, and many times the subject of writing a book would come up. Well, this was the perfect time. I signed the deal in late May, and I have been writing ever since. I initially thought the Yosemite trip would be the final story in this first edition. However, as I was writing in early July, I took stock of our situation. My older son would be done working at the end of July, and he planned to fly home for several weeks in August before we had to get him back to school. Hockey, nearly a year-round sport, had a little break in August before school started for my younger son. My wife had enough vacation time accrued to take a week off. I was, of course, unemployed for the time being as I continued to interview. So I checked possible round-trip flights to Las Vegas, and I found that I had enough miles to fly us for free. The choices were limited, and the best flight times I could get were a departure on Saturday, August 9, with a return on Friday, August 15. I polled the family, and they told me to go for it. I had already talked about going back to Utah if we could swing it this year, so this would be the location for the trip.

The 2014 Western Odyssey would break the earlier trip-planning mold in numerous ways. The first difference was the timing, as the trip would occur in August instead of July. The next difference was in the planning. Beginning the process just one month before departure would limit our lodging choices. Furthermore, while there were new places we had not yet been to, there were places and activities we wanted to duplicate from prior trips. In addition, the earlier budgeting techniques I used were pretty much out the window. Despite my current situation, I was determined to pack in as much fun as possible in approximately six days. I spent days planning and came up with a great itinerary, not knowing that much of it would change unexpectedly.

Step one was choosing when we would go. Because of the spontaneity of my planning, flight availability, and the timing of the boys going back to school, the week of August 9 to 15 was our only choice.

Step two was figuring out how we would get there from Pennsylvania. I had the miles, and I was able to secure tickets for the lowest amount of award miles needed for free tickets.

Step three was determining where we were going to visit and on what days. We would arrive in Las Vegas close to midnight on Saturday, August 9, and my first thought was to drive straight to Utah, arriving early Sunday. My wife was initially agreeable to the idea, but when I explained it would actually require us to drive all night, she insisted we get a hotel Saturday night in Vegas. We would then drive to Bryce Canyon on Sunday morning, hike for the day, and head to Canyonlands via Scenic Byway 12 on Monday. Tuesday would include a visit to Arches and the Delicate Arch in particular. We would drive down the eastern side of the state to Monument Valley on Wednesday, continuing on that evening to St. George, Utah. This would allow us to visit Zion again on Thursday, heading even deeper into the Narrows. So the trip route was set—Bryce Canyon National Park, Scenic Byway 12, Canyonlands National Park, Arches National Park, Monument Valley Navajo Tribal Park, and Zion National Park. These places make up some of the amazing beauty of southern Utah, and it was going to be awesome.

Step four was determining where we were going to stay each night. For the first night in Vegas, I initially looked at the Hooters Casino and Resort but settled on the Las Vegas Hotel farther to the north. In-park lodging was nonexistent at this late stage, so I sought desirable alternatives. I found the Quality Inn outside Bryce Canyon for Sunday night. We would be staying two nights in Moab, and the Motel 6 offered a convenient location there. Wednesday and Thursday night would be spent in St. George, and I discovered the Inn on the Cliff to give us a nice view of the landscape.

Step five was adding tours and additional activities on to the location visits. This is where I decided to duplicate past adventures. Most of the trip would be driving and hiking in the parks, but I carved out some time Tuesday morning to repeat the Ephedra's Grotto canyoneering and rappelling tour we had taken in Moab in 2008. The 2012 UTV side-by-side off-road tour in Warner Valley outside of Hurricane, Utah, was such a blast that I booked it again for Thursday.

Step six was choosing certain meals to get a little fancy with. This time around I did not reserve any specific meals. I figured we would basically wing it, but I still budgeted accordingly based on an estimated amount each day.

Step seven was choosing what vehicle we would drive around

in. I settled on a midsize sedan, figuring we would not really need anything more.

Step eight was making sure we had the right supplies. The adults' Merrells were still in pretty good shape after all these years, so the boys had to find comfortable shoes. Hot weather clothing, sunscreen, hats, sunglasses, electronics, etc., were again part of the packing. My older son brought his Mobius camera with a dash mount for the UTV adventure.

Step nine was budgeting for the trip. The worksheet below is adapted from the spreadsheet file I use for all of our major trips. It shows the plans for the schedule, locations, activities, estimated costs and miles, actual costs, and the timing of the payments for each item. This time around the costs would all hit the same credit card billing cycle.

		2014 TRAVEL COSTS FOR OUR FUN				
DATES	**DESTINATION**	**ITEM**	**ESTIMATES**	**ACTUAL**	**DATES**	**MILES**
08/14	West swing V	Flights — add'l costs	40.00	40.00		
08/14	West swing V	Lodging — Vegas	150.00	278.54		125
08/14	West swing V	Lodging — Bryce Quality Inn	150.00	166.89		280
08/14	West swing V	Lodging — Moab	150.00			
08/14	West swing V	Lodging — Moab	150.00			
08/14	West swing V	Lodging — St. George	150.00	278.74		140
08/14	West swing V	Lodging — St. George	150.00	0.00		
08/14	West swing V	Lodging — St. George	0.00	296.58		230
08/14	West swing V	Lodging — St. George	0.00	0.00		
08/14	West swing V					
08/14	West swing V	RZRs Half Day	600.00	807.45		
08/14	West swing V	Ephedra's Grotto	430.00			
08/14	West swing V	Rental Car	250.00	194.52		
08/14	West swing V	Golf		129.00		
08/14	West swing V	Miles Estimate — 1,500				
08/14	West swing V	Park Fees	40.00	50.00		
08/14	West swing V	Meals estimate 08/10-08/15 (est. $100/day)	600.00	495.38		
08/14	West swing V	Misc. Food	150.00	209.91		
08/14	West swing V	Misc., Nick Knacks, Shirts, Stuff	150.00	277.81		
08/14	West swing V	Gas (estimate 25 mpg x $3.75 x total miles)	225.00	145.73		
08/14	West swing V	Cash — Initial	350.00	350.00		
08/14	West swing V	Cash — ATMs on trip	0.00			
08/14	West swing V	Parking — Airport	56.00	52.00		
Aug Visa	3,422.55	Totals	$3,791.00	$3,772.55		775
Pre-						
Cash	350.00					
	3,772.55					

THE TRIP!

While this was hastily planned and somewhat short on days, my fondness for Utah would be rewarded with a packed agenda. My, how things change. I was really looking forward to seeing Canyonlands since we had bypassed it back in 2008. I was anxious to actually hike to and touch Delicate Arch this time around. I was also excited about Monument Valley, as we had never been there and it seemed to pop up in so many advertisements and movies. These new experiences were wiped out by a phone call and an e-mail. In late July I had a phone interview with a company, and they wanted to bring me in to meet the head of international IT. She was coming in from England, and as luck would have it, the only time she could come was during the week of August 11 to 15. This presented a major quandary because it was a promising and desirable opportunity, but I would be in Utah. We scheduled a Wednesday interview, so I had to figure out how to get home and back to Utah to enjoy some of my vacation. I was able to use credit card miles, but the only feasible airport in Utah was the St. George airport. I found a flight out Tuesday afternoon with a return flight Thursday morning. This effectively eliminated traveling north to Canyonlands and Arches, and Monument Valley was too far east to realistically get to. This forced me to scramble. I cancelled the hotel and the canyoneering adventure in Moab. I then made St. George our home base and added two nights at the Inn on the Cliff. This still left us with time for Bryce Canyon and Zion National Parks along with the Hurricane UTV tour. There was one very small silver lining. We would have much less driving to do. We would make the best of the situation, realizing that any future trips would probably require me to be employed.

Another slight change would be made, but it would be a good one. Near the end of July, I found out our Southern California friends would be staying at the Excalibur hotel in Las Vegas the night of August 9. I cancelled the LVH reservation and told them we would come to meet them and leave around three in the morning. This was before my wife insisted we get a room, so we made it official that we would be staying at the Excalibur too. I also made a switch to the UTV tour time, changing it from Thursday to Friday morning. However, after additional thought and discussions I switched it back to Thursday afternoon following my return flight from Pennsylvania. This would allow us to relax Friday and not worry about getting back to Las Vegas too late.

Saturday, August 9, was here. We were all excited about heading back out west. The airline had numerous hubs where connecting flights meet, and this one would be Dulles in Washington just like two years ago. In the backs of our minds we remembered 2012, so my older son took sinus precautions and promised everything would be fine. The flight left Pittsburgh just before six in the evening, and we were on our way. We encountered no issues on the first flight, and the flight to Vegas, while long, went well. We landed just after ten o'clock, but the rental car counter was a very busy. We eventually got to the hotel near midnight, and we met our friends, heading down for some food, conversation, and wandering around. We had fun until around two in the morning, and everyone headed to bed. My wife, however, was actually wide awake. So we decided to go sightseeing. We walked across Tropicana and explored the New York New York casino. We headed across the Strip to the MGM Grand and north toward shops and lights. It was still bustling, and we enjoyed the hot, dry air. We circled back toward our hotel, stopping to take some pictures. Back at the Excalibur, we decided to strike it rich and do some gambling. It is amazing how quickly you can lose a lot of money on video poker and slots. We cut our losses around four o'clock and went to bed.

We had about five hours to drive Sunday, so we had breakfast with our friends and said our good-byes. It was on to Bryce Canyon. I-15 runs prominently right through the heart of Las Vegas, but you might be surprised how difficult it is to get on it if you make a few wrong turns. I was not lost. I was sightseeing. We finally hit the highway and made our way northeast. It was a beautiful day, but the weather report was showing some rain in the Bryce Canyon area of Utah. We were still excited to get there, and we enjoyed the northwest Arizona mountains before we headed through St. George, Utah. We continued on, opting to stay on I-15 until heading east on Utah Highway 20. This took us through some beautiful mountains, forests, farmland, and curvy roads on our way down to US-89. It also took us through some rain showers that we were hoping would stay to the north. The Quality Inn at Bryce Canyon is listed with a Panguitch address, so we headed south through the town. We passed through it and found the inn just before the beginning of Scenic Byway 12. It was early afternoon, and we were able to check in. This was a nice location, and the guest buildings were separate dual-level structures with eight rooms in each. We were on the second floor of the Stallions building. We unloaded and then set out for Bryce Canyon National Park about twenty miles away. We turned east on Scenic Byway 12, driving through Red Canyon and the picturesque red rock structures and tunnels. This was a nice way to get prepared for the Navajo sandstone formations in Bryce Canyon.

We turned south on Highway 63 and made our way past the commercial area to the park entrance. We used the National Park Service park brochure and the park newspaper guide *The Hoodoo* for reference. We had been there before, and the lodge looked familiar when we arrived. My goal was to do something new, and that meant hiking different trails deeper into the canyon. They do not sell bottled water, so we purchased two refillable water bottles and filled them at the water-filling station in the lodge. We set out on the short trails to the rim of the canyon and started to take in the beauty we had first been introduced to six years before. Since we had only been on one main trail in 2008, I chose a longer one for the afternoon hike. We walked up to Sunrise Point and paused for some pictures, and then we headed north along the rim to the Fairyland Loop Trail. We were not going to make the full eight-mile round trip, but we planned to head out to Tower Bridge and then double back. This moderate hike would take us to dinnertime. We descended down the trail, mindful of the storm clouds gathering above us to the north and west. We encountered plants, Bristlecone Pines, critters, hoodoo rock formations of varying sizes, and colorful sandy slopes. The sandstone is very soft, and the wind, water, and ice have all worked to produce amazing shapes and colors. My younger son, the one who injured himself going off trail here in 2008, was very adventurous. He found numerous alternative routes as we went along, and he did not hesitate to climb rocks, trees, and slopes.

Bryce Canyon National Park

After a short time it started to rain, but to our good fortune, the rain did not last long. We continued on, spying the China Wall from multiple vantage points, and we even saw it through open portals in massive walls of rock. The tan, pink, yellow, and orange sandstone was speckled with green from shrubs and trees. Some of the trees had grown into contorted, spiral shapes, and they were really cool to see and touch. With the sun behind the cloud cover, the earthen colors of the park gave us a new perspective as we soaked in the sights. We were virtually alone on the trail, and as we finally turned around, we had to go uphill. We were up to the task, stopping as needed in order to explore, take pictures, drink water, and enjoy the scenery. We made our way to the lodge and were able to get a table for dinner. It was here that I reunited with an old favorite. I ordered a Cutthroat Pale Ale from the Uinta Brewing Company. After dinner we walked back to the rim of the canyon and Sunset Point, making our way through throngs of photographers. We were in luck, as the clouds had dissipated and the super moon was upon us. We took pictures and thought about heading down the Navajo Loop Trail. After one or two switchbacks, we realized we were too full from dinner, so we made our way back to the car. We drove back to the

Quality Inn and enjoyed our room for the night. I took some pictures and video of the super moon before I went to sleep.

My updated plan for Monday included a quick hike in Bryce Canyon and a trek to Calf Creek Falls on Scenic Byway 12. However, after we assessed the time involved to get to Calf Creek Falls, we decided on the Bryce Canyon hike only. After I watched the sunrise, we checked out and headed back through Red Canyon on our way to the park. We made our way to the lodge and then out to the canyon rim. We found our way back to the trail we enjoyed so much in 2008. We entered the Navajo Loop Trail, but this time we would go clockwise. After we filled our water bottles, we started our descent for the midmorning hike. The sun was out, brightening the orange rocks and casting shadows along the way. We saw familiar sights and landmarks, and we explored areas that were new to us. We headed down the switchbacks as my son found creative ways to get to the same destination as the rest of us. It was a beautiful day, and the altitude kept the temperature comfortable as we hiked. We climbed trees, rocks, and slopes, sometimes posing for pictures that were remakes of the same poses from six years prior. Of course, most of us were bigger now. After a couple of hours we climbed the switchbacks to the end of the trail. I was stopped by a Japanese lady asking for trail directions. Being the experienced hiker and master of communications, I think I pointed her and her companions in the right direction. At least I hoped so. We said good-bye to Bryce Canyon and headed back to US-89 South. We decided to head toward our hotel in St. George, taking Highway 9 West to I-15. This would take us right by Zion National Park.

Since it was still early and Zion was less than two hours away, we decided to make that our second stop of the day. Two years earlier we hiked the Narrows, but we did not get as far as we could have. The decision this day was to go in farther, hopefully to Orderville Canyon. We made our way west on Highway 9, enjoying the increasing beauty. We were behind two bikers who stopped suddenly at one point. We stopped and then looked up at what they were fixated on. There were three mountain goats perched high on the rocks above us, and one seemed to defy gravity as it walked up the side of the rock. This was really cool. We took pictures and then made our way to the Zion-Mount Carmel

Tunnel. We had to wait to be let through, and when our turn came, we drove through the darkness, quickly looking out the right side through the holes cut in the mountainside. We weaved our way through the slick rock and red slopes to the visitor center parking lot. Since we were not staying at the lodge, we had to take the shuttle into the park. There had been quite a bit of rain here recently, and the possibility of flash flooding in the Narrows was not ruled out. We stopped at the Zion Lodge and grabbed some lunch. We filled our water bottles and took the shuttle directly to the Temple of Sinawava. We were fixated on the Narrows this time, and we walked the river walk trail to the water's edge.

Just like our last time here, we had to walk through some fast-moving water over slippery rocks. There were low spots, rocky shores, paths, rocks to climb, and variable currents to navigate. Despite the recent rains, the water was actually a little lower than the last time we were here. We continued our trek up the Virgin River, and we soon got to the point where we turned around in 2012. We were not letting up, and we found places with new features, colors, and shapes. We plodded through some more difficult sections and explored the new places with vigor. Some corners brought noticeably cool breezes, while others took us briefly into the dark. The canyon walls rose higher and higher around us, offering gorgeous patterns and colors. There were more people than I had expected in the slot canyon, but the numbers dwindled as we moved up the river. We had some memorable experiences in the water and behind the rocks as we explored. I knew we would not get to Orderville Canyon, so after every big turn, we assessed what was ahead to see if we wanted to keep going. After a number of "just a little longer" choices, the sun disappeared, and light rain made its way into the slot. We were not too concerned, but after a quick series of lightning flashes above the canyon walls, we decided it was time to turn back. I continued to take some pictures, but I was ordered to stow the camera and get moving just in case. The trip back to the river walk went pretty quick, and we made our way down to the shuttle stop. We did what we could to expel the sand from our shoes and socks, and we boarded the shuttle. After we got back to the car, we changed and headed to St. George. We checked into the hotel and then went to dinner at a nearby Tex-Mex restaurant.

Zion National Park—The Narrows

This is where my trip took a kind of hiatus. I had to be at the St. George airport around noon on Tuesday to fly home for my Wednesday interview in New York. We would be staying at the Inn on the Cliff the rest of the week, and it turned out to be a great place for us. The view was beautiful, and the staff was accommodating to our changing needs. My wife and sons would be without me from Tuesday afternoon until noon Thursday. They went golfing, shopping, eating, and swimming, and they watched *Shark Week*. They drove back to Zion briefly and checked out some of the many state parks near St. George. They basically relaxed, using the hotel pool and enjoying their freedom from me. I am sure they missed me.

I had to be at the Pittsburgh airport around five thirty Thursday morning. The flight stopped in Denver before it took me to the long St. George runway. My family picked me up, and we headed to Hurricane for our afternoon four-hour UTV adventure in Warner Valley. It was a marvelous day, and we got some burritos for lunch before we headed to the Southern Utah Adventure Center. The owner remembered us from

2012, and he got us prepped for the fun. He had done us a favor with the repeated rescheduling of our tour. Unlike the last time, our guide was combining our two UTVs with another family in a four-seater model. They would follow the guide, and we would be the number-three and -four vehicles. The recent rain had dried up, so we would not get muddy like last time. We outfitted ourselves with goggles and bandanas for the dust we would encounter. The boys would be the first drivers, and we set out from the shop through the streets of Hurricane. School had already started there, so we passed kids on their way home from school.

After a couple of miles, we entered the dirt trails into Warner Valley, anticipating the fun. After only about a half hour, my younger son managed to accomplish what we pretty much thought could not be done. He blew out our right front tire. There was a large rock in one of the ruts, and it had a jagged edge jutting out. It caught the sidewall of our tire and ripped a gash in it. I noticed it and told him to stop. Since we were the last UTV, the others continued on without knowing we had stopped. I jumped on the back and started waving while my son ran back to check out the rock that did us in. Finally I saw our guide coming back to us, and after he surveyed the situation, he called the shop to deliver a new tire. He left again to resume the tour for the others. We had water, but it was really hot that day. It took more than a half hour for the other guide to get to us, and we changed the tire after some effort. He gave us more water and then led us to the fort where the others were waiting. We got going again, but I was disappointed because we missed out on the purple moon mounds, where we had had so much fun the last time. Fortunately the valley was large, and since this was a different guide than the last time, we found new places and new trails. We zigzagged through passes and rock walls, speeding up when the trails allowed us to. We hit ruts and mounds, getting airborne on a few occasions.

After another brief stop, we switched up, and I drove with my older son for a while. His dashboard-mounted Mobius camera took some excellent footage of our drive. We eventually made it to the base of a steep sand dune. One by one, we backed up the hill behind us and gunned it down and then up to get to the top. Two of the drivers took multiple attempts before they got to the summit. My younger son was with my wife in the more powerful UTV, and he got up the hill without a problem. I figured I would have no problem, and about ten feet from the top I spun us out and got stuck. I had to slowly back all the way down and start again. After three of these futile runs and my son calling me all kinds of dork-related names, I noticed a path up to the left that was not quite as steep. I gunned it up there, and we made it to the top. We were back in business. The group spent a lot of time in the sand, and we did patterns, curves, jumps, hill hairpins, and straights. We stopped for a break on top of a mesa, and we could see way down into the valley behind us. The tracks going up a steep hill were in the distance. I paired up with my younger son and took the helm of the 900cc machine for a short time. After we hit some more dunes, I let him finish up. We flew over more hills and left the sand in our wake as we made our way above the Sand Hollow Reservoir. Finally it was time to head back to the shop, so we descended to the road below. My son took turns falling behind and seeing what speed he could get the UTV up to, briefly eclipsing seventy miles per hour. We got back to the Southern Utah Adventure Center location in Hurricane and unloaded. We thanked the guide and the owner for yet another entertaining outing in the desert. If we get back near Hurricane in the future, SUAC will be high on our list again.

08/14/2014

Hurricane, Utah—UTV Side by Sides in Warner Valley

We headed west and south back to the hotel, stopping for some supplies. I was in the mood for a beer, and I looked for the remedy at a drugstore. I was in luck, and I found a four-pack of Dead Horse Amber Ale from the Moab Brewery. We never did make it to Moab on this trip, but this was a nice treat from that excellent town. With an hour or so of sun left, we headed to the pool to cool off and relax. After that, we decided to stay put and have dinner at the hotel's Cliffside Restaurant. Along with a great view of the city and mountains beyond, the food was very good, and we retired to the room for our last night of vacation. We did not have anything new planned for Friday morning, so my wife and I went to the pool while the boys slept. We met a very nice couple from New York and swapped stories with them while we swam and sat in the hot tub. I still had some Dead Horse left from the night before, so this was the perfect time to crack one open. My older son came to the pool for a short while, but it was time for us to shower, pack up, and check out.

We only had about a two- to three-hour drive to Vegas, and our flight was not until 5:50 p.m. We stopped for lunch, and I celebrated as they took me to an Einstein Bros Bagels restaurant they had found while I was away. We gassed up and headed southwest one more time. I again expressed my adulation for the fourteen-mile stretch of mountains as we passed through Arizona's northwest corner. We blew through Mesquite and got to Las Vegas with plenty of time to spare. I filled the tank one last time on this sweltering afternoon, and we dropped off the rental car. We took the shuttle to the terminal, and I noticed I had one more Dead Horse in the backpack. It was pretty warm; however, this was Vegas, and I could not just pour it out. Tasty.

We made it to our gate and took turns wandering the airport as we waited for our flight. This first leg was going to Chicago, so neither flight would be excessively long. On the flight I gazed out the window as long as there was light, seeing some pretty cool sights from thirty thousand feet. At one point I could see a fireworks show in the distance, and it looked like tiny little explosions of sparks below us. We got to Chicago near midnight central time, but our flight to Pittsburgh was not until 6:30 a.m. This was a minor pain, as these airport benches were not as comfortable as some we had slept on before. We made it home on Saturday morning, and we relaxed in our own beds and on our own floor.

SUMMATION

Western Odyssey #5 was now history. Although it was planned on the fly, it had the makings of another classic vacation. An unforeseen turn of events partially blunted that hope. We still made the best of it, and we had a great time in southern Utah. While this was somewhat a repeat adventure, it was different in a number of ways. The original plan that included Bryce Canyon National Park, Scenic Byway 12 through Capitol Reef National Park, Canyonlands National Park, Arches National Park, Monument Valley, and Zion National Park was a great one even packed into one week. We still found new trails in Bryce Canyon, went farther into the Narrows in Zion, experienced more UTV exhilaration in Hurricane, and found some cool lodging unrelated to the parks to make this abbreviated trip one of the most memorable ever! Missing out on Canyonlands again was disappointing; however, now I have a reason to go back, and the third time will be a charm. Oh, and I did not end up getting the job in New York, as it would have relocated me 150 miles away from home. I will keep working on that effort, and I will keep planning more trips. The year 2016 is coming up quickly, after all.

Family at Bryce Canyon National Park

EPILOGUE

This is the end of my family's travel chronicles ... for now. I have had a fantastic time planning the itineraries, and we have had rewarding experiences taking these journeys to far-off destinations. Unless otherwise noted, all of the places mentioned here still exist based on recent research. There are more than four hundred official units of the National Park System. Of these there are fifty-nine national parks and seventy-nine national monuments. We still have a long way to go to experience them all, but over the last eight years the parks, monuments, and other places we have chosen for our trips comprise an awesome collection of the American landscape. We have seen breathtaking sights, met great people, stayed in unique lodging, eaten fabulous food, watched our boys grow, and collected a multitude of memories. You can see that my family loves to have fun, take some risks, be adventurous, and get back to nature whenever possible. We have seen some and missed some, but sometimes just standing on the edge of a canyon and gazing down into it is enough to stimulate your senses and etch a memory for life. We have touched the surfaces of places called Acadia, Badlands, Glacier, Olympic, Yosemite, and Zion, just to name a few. Create your own masterpieces and compare your stories to ours. Whether it is a river, a trail, a rock, a road, a canyon, a mountain, a glacier, or a craft beer, we want you to be able to say "I was there", and be inspired to create and enjoy your own best trip(s) ever! The more time you can spend at any of these places, the better. I would love to exchange more photographs and stories with you sometime. Maybe we could enjoy a beer together. Any one of these would be a welcome refreshment:

Grand Teton Brewing Company	Bitch Creek ESB	2006/2008
Uinta Brewing Company	Cutthroat Pale Ale	2008/2012/2014
Shipyard Brewing Company	Shipyard Export Ale	2009
Harpoon Brewery	Harpoon IPA	2009
Redhook Brewing Company	Redhook ESB	2010
Big Sky Brewing Company	Trout Slayer Ale	2010
Mammoth Brewing Company	Ahwahnee Amber Ale	2012
Moab Brewing Company	Dead Horse Amber Ale	2014

I also encourage you to get on mailing lists of the places you like. I still receive e-mails from the Yellowstone Park Foundation, Kalaloch Lodge, Sorrel River Ranch, Southern Utah Adventure Center, the Luxor, Glacier Park, and the Furnace Creek Resort, among others. These are but a few of the places I hope to get back to when I finally become a professional park-goer, volunteer, park ranger, or something like that.

I want to mention one more destination that is not described in the trip chapters. Since 2006, we have been visiting Washington, DC, multiple times a year to support our favorite charity, *The Aleethia Foundation*. This organization assists wounded troops, and we show our support in person as often as possible. When we visit, we also try to spend time at the museums, monuments, the National Mall, military memorials, and one of the most awe-inspiring places anywhere: Arlington National Cemetery. As you may already know, our nation's capital is a must-see destination for many reasons, so definitely try to add it to your list.

These trip chapters are not exhaustive reference guides with a large amount of technical information. You can obtain that from many sources during your research, including *Fodor's, Frommer's, Lonely Planet, TripAdvisor, National Geographic, Xanterra, National Park Reservations, REI*, and the National Park Service, to name just a few. My goal here is to inspire you with ideas, enlighten you with experiences, and entertain you with personal stories. I get personal gratification when my family shares laughs and tells me how much fun they had somewhere on a trip. If you can possibly find the time, try to see as many of these places at different times of the day and different seasons of the year. Pick up an atlas, download some NPS brochures and park newspapers, and come along with us. If you have been to any of these locations, you may know more about them than I do. If you have not, then I hope you find something here that excites you and motivates you to go. Regardless, whether you are a first-timer or a veteran, I hope this encourages you to plan, take, and share *Your Best Trip Ever!*